I0949745

FINAL DAWN
OVER JERUSALEM

JOHN HAGEE

THOMAS NELSON PUBLISHERS
Nashville

Copyright © 1998 by John C. Hagee

All rights reserved. Written permission must be secured from the publisher to use or reproduce any part of this book, except for brief quotations in critical reviews or articles.

Published in Nashville, Tennessee, by Thomas Nelson, Inc., Publishers.

The Bible version used in this publication is THE NEW KING JAMES VERSION. Copyright © 1979, 1980, 1982, Thomas Nelson, Inc., Publishers.

Library of Congress Cataloging-in-Publication Data

Hagee, John C.
    Final dawn over Jerusalem : the world's future hangs in the balance with the battle for the holy city / John Hagee.
        p. cm.
    Includes bibliographical references.
    ISBN 0-7852-7083-3
    1. Bible—Prophecies—Jerusalem.   2. Jerusalem in the Bible.
I. Title.
BS649.J38H34
220.1'5—dc21   97-41205
                                                          CIP

Printed in the United States of America.
1 2 3 4 5 6 BVG 03 02 01 00 99 98

Lovingly dedicated to my children:
Tish, Christopher, Christina, Matthew, and Sandra

CONTENTS

Foreword   *ix*

Part I
The People of Jerusalem

1. Jerusalem, City of Peace   *3*

2. He Who Blesses Israel...   *18*

3. He Who Curses Israel...   *34*

4. The Crucifixion of the Jews   *43*

5. Who Really Killed Christ?   *76*

6. Has God Rejected the Jews?   *95*

Part II
The Prophecies of Jerusalem

7. Jerusalem the Golden   *127*

8. Winds of War over Jerusalem   *139*

9. Glimpses of the Future   *162*

10. The Final Dawn over Jerusalem   *193*

Notes   *207*

About the Author   *213*

FOREWORD

The English statesman and author Benjamin Disraeli once said, "The view of Jerusalem is the history of the world; it is more, it is the history of earth and of heaven."[1]

I'd like to amend Disraeli's astute comment—in a view of Jerusalem we uncover more than the *history* of the world, we also discover the *forecast*. In Jerusalem we can find the key to the future of the universe and the hope of all mankind. One day in the not-too-distant future a king will come, the promised Messiah. Then Jew and Gentile alike will see Him walk upon the streets of Jerusalem. Together we will shout for joy as we look upon the King of kings, and the Lord of lords.

The Messiah for whose coming we yearn will establish a kingdom of lasting peace—how fitting that His capitol will be Jerusalem, whose very name means "city of peace." As the nations of the world cry out for peace, the winds of war are gathering over the ancient city of Jerusalem. The sun—the God-ordained timekeeper that has faithfully risen and set over that beloved site since time began—will descend behind the Holy City's walls one last time. And in the morning, when that final day dawns over Jerusalem, the King of kings will establish His kingdom. The Chosen People, the Seed of Abraham, will welcome their Messiah, and He will be the Lamp of the City and the Light of the World.

I have a deep and abiding love for Jerusalem. I made my first visit to that Holy City in April 1979, when as a goy tourist preacher I walked through those ancient streets and marveled at the beauty of the city and the spirit of its people. I could not write about the war and desolation to come without a broken heart unless I had the confidence to also write about the victorious final chapter in Jerusalem's history. Darkness will come, and it will be the darkest night in Israel's history. But with the morning come great joy and the final dawn.

Jerusalem will greet its Messiah. At the dawning of that day, the Messiah will rule the world with truth and grace. He will make the nations prove the glories of His righteousness and the wonders of His love.

Come with me as we explore this Holy City and the chosen people of God who stand to inherit it. If we are to understand *why* God will do what He is planning to do in the future, we must understand *the people* through whom He has chosen to work.

The dawning of Jerusalem's glory is not far away.

PART I

THE
PEOPLE
OF
JERUSALEM

CHAPTER 1

JERUSALEM, CITY OF PEACE

June 7, 1981, began like any quiet Sunday in Washington, D.C. A hot afternoon sun flooded the Rose Garden behind the White House and lit the white pillars of that stately residence. Nothing seemed amiss; President and Mrs. Reagan were away at Camp David for a restful weekend retreat.

But in his office, National Security Adviser Richard V. Allen was trying to stifle his panic as he telephoned the president. An aide answered the phone at Camp David and told Allen that the president had just boarded the helicopter for the return trip to Washington. "Get him off the chopper," Allen said bluntly. "It's imperative that I speak to him at once."

"You've got to be kidding. The chopper's already revved up—"

"Get him off."

Moments later the president took the phone. As helicopter blades whirred and chopped in the background, Allen explained that the Israelis had just taken out a nuclear reactor in Iraq. "They used American F-16s, sir. We sold those seventy-five F-16s with the stipulation that they be used only for defensive purposes."

"What do you know about it?" asked the president.

"Nothing, sir. I'm waiting for a report."

"Why do you suppose they did it?"

Allen mulled the question for a moment. "Well, sir . . . boys will be boys."[1]

Objective: Osirak

At 4:40 P.M. Israeli time, a secret squadron had left underground bunkers at Israel's Etzion air base in the Sinai. The formation of flyers crossed the Gulf of 'Aqaba and flew over Jordan. Taking advantage of blind spots in the Arab radar system, the fourteen aircraft stayed close to the ground. To deceive any radio intervention, each pilot spoke flawless Arabic.

Back in Jerusalem, Israeli cabinet members were assembling at Menachem Begin's private residence in the Rehavya suburbs. Each official had been summoned by private invitation, and each stepped into the reception area only to discover himself among a group of confused and curious colleagues. The officials were soon shocked to hear that they were part of a clandestine meeting.

At 5:15 P.M. Begin emerged from his private office with astounding news. The prime minister, casually dressed in shirtsleeves, calmly announced, "Several of our planes are now on their way to their target in Iraq. I hope our boys will be able to complete their mission successfully and return to base."[2]

As the sun set over Baghdad, six F-15 camouflaged interceptors fell into a protective formation above eight F-16s carrying 2,000-pound bombs. The timing had been carefully orchestrated to minimize the possibility of injuring

Iraqi civilians at the reactor site. At the agreed-upon time, the Israeli jets dropped out of the sky, blasting the nuclear reactor station at Osirak.

When the lead plane released the first salvo, video-guided "smart" bombs blew holes in the concrete barriers around the reactors. No one would find the remains of the homing device that ensured that the missiles went straight to their target. The device had been hidden in a briefcase planted earlier by an agent of the Israeli secret service, Mossad. After the first explosions, the roof of the reactor collapsed, sending hundreds of tons of concrete and steel crashing to earth. Within moments, the Iraqi's $260 million nuclear-research reactor and all of its technical equipment became a smoking rubble. Saddam Hussein's ability to build an atomic bomb was crushed for the moment.

Two Israeli F-16s made a final pass to photograph the destruction. Complete desolation was confirmed, with one civilian casualty. With their mission accomplished, the squadron began the fifty-minute return flight home.

In Jerusalem, the stunned cabinet members assembled at Begin's residence gained their composure and debated how they should respond if one of their planes was shot down. Shortly before 7:00 P.M., a phone call reported the safe return of every plane. The jubilant assembly applauded and celebrated. Within a few moments, Begin lifted the phone and telephoned the U.S. ambassador to Israel to explain the raid.

Ambassador Samuel Lewis's reply to the news that American-supplied jets had just struck Iraq? "You don't say."

Not every reaction was so laconic. TASS, the Soviet news agency, immediately labeled the raid an "act of gangsterism" and accused the United States of complicity. Egypt's former prime minister warned that the time was approaching to take action against Israel. Arab League Secretary General Chedli Klibi demanded U.N. sanctions against Israel.

On Monday morning, leading figures in the Reagan administration met to assess the situation. Vice President George Bush and Chief of Staff Jim Baker urged significant sanctions against Israel. Secretary of Defense Caspar Weinberger wanted to cancel further F-16 sales. President Reagan was personally pleased with the Israelis, believing that their willingness to use force was the most effective path to peace. In the end, however, the White House released a terse, harsh statement criticizing the action, condemning the attack, and threatening punitive response. The State Department said the surprise raid "cannot but seriously add to the already tense situation in the area."

Menachem Begin answered immediately. "The Iraqis were preparing atomic bombs to drop on the children of Israel," he told the world. "Haven't you heard of one and a half million little Jewish children who were thrown into the gas chambers?" He did not hesitate to employ passionate rhetoric. "Another Holocaust would have happened in the history of the Jewish people. Never again, never again. Tell your friends, tell anybody you meet, we shall defend our people with all the means at our disposal."

Despite Begin's eloquent defense of his actions, a cartel of nations pressed for retribution. After six days of debate at the United Nations, Ambassador Jeane J. Kirkpatrick voted against America's staunch friend Israel, saying, "The means Israel chose to quiet its fears have hurt, not helped, the peace and security of the area." Ambassador Kirkpatrick joined fifteen other members of the U.N. Security Council and condemned the Israeli raid. An Arab diplomat analyzed the vote by saying, "The United States saved face in the Middle East. The Iraqis won a moral victory."[3]

In the days that followed, the Begin government published several previously classified facts. Over thirteen feet beneath the demolished reactor, the Iraqis maintained a secret installation for use in developing an atomic weapon. The Iraqis had also stockpiled 200 tons of natural uranium called *yellowcake,* the deadly powder used to create plutonium. Tiny Israel knew it could not survive a first-strike nuclear attack. Every military base would be gone in one blast. Anticipatory self-defense was the only intelligent option for survival.

In subsequent weeks, newspapers across the world blasted Israel in column after column of bitter denunciation. The American Congress held special hearings and suspended further sales of F-16s to Israel. While popular at home, Menachem Begin became a pariah in the eyes of the world. His description of Saddam Hussein as an evil ruler was universally rejected.

Saddam Hussein Unveiled

A decade later, the sons and daughters of American citizens joined with troops from across the world to stop Hussein's sudden, devastating attack on Kuwait. With his sophisticated Iraqi army, Hussein destroyed oil wells and crushed the small country's meager military resources. Hussein, the "victim" of the Osirak raid, had acquired a new image as the madman of the Middle East. The nations in the Security Council who had so vehemently condemned the Israeli attack found themselves forced to change their opinions about Middle East aggressors. Menachem Begin now appeared to be a prophet.

Americans were slow to realize the full ramifications of that hot, quiet afternoon in June 1981. If Israel had not destroyed Hussein's atomic bomb factory, thousands of America's finest and best would have been slaughtered in a nuclear holocaust in the desert.

The secret raid at sundown had saved the world from an Armageddon appointment.

I remember reading the screaming headlines of *The New York Times:* ISRAELI JETS DESTROY IRAQ ATOMIC REACTOR—ATTACK CONDEMNED BY U.S. AND ARAB NATIONS. The gripping account of Israel's preemptive strike on Hussein's atomic reactor was also front-page news in San Antonio. I read the articles with a grim expression, knowing that Hussein's frantic attempts to develop weapons of mass destruction were for only one diabolical end—Iraq intended to blow Jerusalem off the map.

Excellent, I thought as I read. *Israel struck first, just like you'd shoot a coiled rattlesnake on the front porch. You wouldn't wait to see if the serpent was bluffing.*

Israel knows that the Hitlers, Stalins, Ayatollah Khomeinis, Husseins, and other lunatics of the world must be taken seriously. The Israeli Defense Force (IDF) action upon Osirak was simple and logical. If more countries took evil as seriously as Israel, the Hitlers of history would not have the opportunity to accumulate enough power to drag the world into a bloodbath.

I turned to the editorial page of the San Antonio paper, expecting to find an enthusiastic endorsement of Israel, but I was shocked. Our best ally in that volatile part of the globe was the target of several scathing attacks. My local newspaper condemned Israel as being as aggressive as Libya. I was deeply disturbed about my local paper's position. I sought out other national newspapers and discovered more of the same. The American media was in a feeding frenzy, and the State of Israel was the only item on the menu.

From deep within my soul, a trumpet sounded. I knew I could not stand idly by and let this moment, this unjust criticism, pass unchallenged. I reminded myself of a familiar Edmund Burke quote: "The only thing necessary for the triumph of evil is for good men to do nothing."

A Cradle-Roll Zionist

My support for the State of Israel began at our family altar. For fifty years, my father was a minister of the gospel and a Bible scholar. Many evenings our family gathered around the dining table as my father taught us from the Bible that the Jewish people were "the apple of God's eye." He taught the members of his congregation that the nation of Israel is God's prophetic timepiece for the ages. He taught that Jerusalem, the city of God, would be the focal point of the world from this moment until the coming of the Messiah.

During the darkest days of World War II, Dad kept reminding his congregants that they would see the day when the State of Israel would be reborn "in a day." On May 15, 1948, we were in our kitchen listening to the radio when the greatest political miracle of the twentieth century became a reality. Our family sat mesmerized as my father's teachings passed from prophecy into history. The birth of the State of Israel confirmed the accuracy of Bible prophecy and was God's notary seal on my father's ministry.

In April 1979 I took my first trip to Israel. I walked in the steps of Christ from His birth in Bethlehem, His baptism in the Jordon, His betrayal by Judas in Gethsemane, and His brilliant resurrection at the Garden Tomb. I sailed across the Sea of Galilee, the same sea my Savior traversed in the midst of a raging storm to calm His terrified disciples. I stood at the rocky crest of Calvary and marveled at the miracle of redemption.

Though I was tremendously excited about my pilgrimage, nothing prepared me for the beauty of the land and the spirit of the people. The accomplishments of Jewish sweat, blood, tears, and genius had changed the desert into a garden, poverty into prosperity, a forsaken wilderness into a wonderland.

Barren mountains had become forests of green. Malaria-infested swamps had disappeared to make way for groves of eucalyptus trees. A dispossessed people had turned a damaged land into everything promised by the prophet Isaiah.

Struggling through unbearable obstacles at incalculable personal cost, doctors, lawyers, professors, merchants, and musicians speaking more than sixty languages abandoned their European heritages and prosperous lifestyles to reconstitute the nation promised to Abraham. With the blood of King David flowing in their veins, these pioneers came back once again to banish the local Goliaths. With not much more firepower than David's slingshot, they faced Arabs armed to the teeth by the British. Not giving an inch, the dispossessed became the masters of what had been Palestine.

This land, promised to Abraham, Isaac, and Jacob, was theirs forever through the unconditional and unbreakable blood covenant expressed in Genesis: "On the same day the LORD made a covenant with Abram, saying: 'To your descendants I have given this land, from the river of Egypt to the great river, the River Euphrates—the Kenites, the Kenezzites, the Kadmonites, the Hittites, the Perizzites, the Rephaim, the Amorites, the Canaanites, the Girgashites, and the Jebusites'" (Gen. 15:18–21).

The courageous enthusiasm of these sons and daughters of Gideon gave birth to modern Israel and magnetically invited their still-wandering relatives to return. The spirit of Theodor Herzl, Chaim Weizmann, Golda Meir, Moshe Dayan, and Menachem Begin surged across the fruited coastal plains and sent my imagination soaring to the heights of Mount Hermon.

I loved the spirit of these people. Since statehood, they have consistently been America's only true friends in the Middle East.

A Time to Act

But while the Iraqi reactor at Osirak smoldered in ruins, many American friends of Israel were ominously quiet. As the American press blasted Israel with scathing denunciations and threats of political reprisal, I felt it was time to stand and speak up. It was time to do something, but what? Instantly a concept exploded in my mind. Why not have a massive public demonstration of support for Israel? Americans are quick to demonstrate for things we are *against,* why not demonstrate for causes we *support*? We would call it "A Night to Honor Israel."

The morning this idea came to me, my wife, Diana, and I sat at the breakfast table, and I shared the concept with her. I reached for pad and pen to put a few thoughts on paper. Maybe other clergy would stand with me, I told Diana. I would send at least 150 letters to other clergymen across San Antonio, inviting them to join me in a public statement and display of support for Israel. We would hold a press conference to announce our intention to convene A Night to Honor Israel. Within a few minutes, everything fell into place . . . on paper.

I had mistakenly thought that most clergymen in San Antonio would be happy to join me, but only one pastor, Dr. Buckner Fanning of Trinity Baptist Church, answered my letter favorably. I soon discovered that anti-Semitism was alive and well in the church that had been founded by a Rabbi who taught "love thy neighbor as thyself."

Strange, isn't it, that we tend to forget that Jesus was Jewish? Too many Christians believe that Jesus was the son of Mr. and Mrs. Christ, that He was born in Bethlehem, and that He later called twelve nice, blond, blue-eyed disciples to help Him found the church.

In any case, I found myself planning a gala night without much support. I soon found my life threatened.

With Dr. Fanning, the pastor who agreed to join me, and two local rabbis, I organized a press conference to announce the upcoming event. We made our statements, the photographers snapped our pictures, and then the fireworks started. Within an hour after the newspapers hit the stand the next morning, someone called a death threat in to my church. "Tell that preacher he'll be dead by Friday!" the caller said.

I take death threats seriously, so I contacted our chief of security and was told to immediately discontinue all my routine activities. "Do not go to the office the same way every day," he told me. "Use a different car, study in a different place, cancel your social engagements, and buy and wear a bulletproof vest." You can be sure I did as I was told.

I had begun to think the threat wasn't serious until the windows of my car were shot out while the vehicle was parked in front of my home. Tension mounted as the date for A Night to Honor Israel drew near.

On September 10, 1981, the Lila Cockrell Theater for the Performing Arts was filled to capacity with friends who wished to honor Israel. All of the San Antonio rabbis were in attendance, as well as myself and the lone Baptist pastor who had joined with me. The rabbis and Buckner Fanning stood with me on the platform as the Cornerstone Church sanctuary choir and orchestra played and sang Hebrew songs in Hebrew (well, *Southern* Hebrew). I smiled and listened to the music, glancing over the crowd, looking for any unusual movements. I was extremely tense, but the evening progressed smoothly.

What we wanted to demonstrate that night wasn't simply support, but love. Love isn't what you say—it's what you *do*. It wasn't enough to express support for Israel and the Jewish people of the world; we knew we had to do something tangible to demonstrate our love. We decided prior to this night to take an offering for Hadassah Hospital in Jerusalem, a medical facility that treats both Jews and Arabs.

After the choir sang so beautifully "Jerusalem of Gold," "Y'Varech'Cha," and other songs, I walked to the lectern and delivered a speech unlike any I had ever given in decades of ministry. "Israel and the Jews have heard the voices of their enemies for centuries," I began. "They have endured untold hardship and persecution, but we are here tonight to say it's time for them to hear the voices of their friends, loud and clear. It's time for courage and conviction to replace cowardice and complacency."

I told them of my pilgrimage to Jerusalem and how I felt a very special presence in that Holy City, the city of God. As I stood on the cobblestone streets of the Old City, I knew I had found my spiritual home.

Next, I addressed the issue of the Israeli air raid on the nuclear reactor at Osirak. "We are here tonight to loudly say that we are not appalled by Israel's defending itself in a climate of war. Rather, we applaud Israel for its courage and determination to give no quarter to terrorists in the Middle East."

I pressed even harder on an issue that is the lifeblood of America's economy—oil. "Sooner or later, the present oil glut will be used up and foreign governments will demand we make a choice," I said. "They will tell us, 'Stop supporting Israel or you'll buy no more oil from the Persian Gulf states!'" I paused and looked over the crowd. "I hope and pray when that day arrives, millions of Americans will stand up and tell the oil monarchs to keep their oil. We'd rather ride bicycles and support the State of Israel!"

The audience was stunned. I don't know what they were expecting me to say, but they obviously weren't expecting that kind of support.

I went on to quote the words of Pastor Martin Neimoller, whose voice from the Nazi era reminded us of the importance of speaking up for right and becoming involved: "When Hitler attacked the Jews I was not a Jew; therefore, I was not concerned. And when Hitler attacked the Catholics, I was not a Catholic, and, therefore, I was not concerned. And when Hitler attacked the unions and the industrialists, I was not a member of the unions, and I was not concerned. Then Hitler attacked me and the Protestant church—and there was nobody left to be concerned."[4]

I closed my speech by reviewing the blessings the Jewish people have brought to America in the fields of education, finance, medicine, music, science, and philanthropy. I also praised the 500,000 Jewish soldiers who served the United States with valor in World War II.

"It is not possible for a man to truthfully say, 'I am a Christian,' and not love the Jewish people," I concluded.

As soon as my speech had ended, we took an offering for Hadassah Hospital.

I presented a four-foot cardboard check for $10,000 to the local president of Hadassah. As I announced the amount of the check to the crowd and to those who would later watch on national television, tears began to flow down the cheeks of the woman to whom I was presenting the gift. A moment later, her tears turned into audible sobs; in an instant, the thousands of people in that auditorium melded together. I scanned the audience and saw some of the most influential citizens of San Antonio openly weeping. I shall always cherish that memory.

Terrorism in San Antonio

After presenting the check, I introduced Rabbi Scheinberg to give the benediction. As he began to pray, an aide slipped to my side and pressed a message into my hand— someone had called a bomb threat into the *San Antonio Express-News* newspaper. Terrorists threatened to blow up the auditorium at 9:30 P.M. My watch said 9:27.

As the rabbi's last words left his mouth, I leaped for the microphone. "I hate to end this lovely evening on a negative note," I said, "but security has informed me that in two minutes a bomb is supposed to explode in this building. Please leave quickly."

Most of the Christians ran for the doors with shock and terror evident on their faces. To my surprise, most of the Jews flipped their hands in traditional Hebrew fashion as if to say, "We've been through this a thousand times. We're not being intimidated by screwballs." Most of my congregation scurried for shelter as I watched. The resolve of the

Jewish community profoundly impressed me. They leisurely greeted their friends, finished their conversations, and took their leave.

Security guards rushed Diana and me out the back door with Zion Evrony, the consul general of Israel. As we were driving back to his hotel, a thunderbolt of righteous anger shot through my soul. "I'm not going to let a Nazi mentality terrorize me into silence and submission," I told Consul General Evrony. "If they want a fight, we'll give them more than they bargained for. If A Night to Honor Israel made them mad, let's see their response to our repeating the event throughout the length and breadth of America."

That night I knew we had to take A Night to Honor Israel across the nation. We would take the choir, the orchestra, and whoever would go to America's great metropolitan centers. My intention was to stand against anti-Semitism in the church and in the bloodstream of America until the vipers that made the threatening phone calls slithered back into the sewer.

We took A Night to Honor Israel to Houston, Austin, Dallas, Fort Worth, Phoenix, Los Angeles, and Tulsa, where goose-stepping skinheads marched down the street in front of the auditorium in full Nazi uniform, screaming, "Seig Heil" while carrying signs that read, WHO PAYS JOHN HAGEE?

One of the highlights of my life was taking A Night to Honor Israel to Jerusalem. Transporting a 200-voice choir with full orchestra was expensive, but our people believed in this effort. Some sold the furniture out of their homes, and others sold their second cars to raise money for the trip. After months of fund-raising, we had the necessary finances. We boarded an El Al jet, and on wings of eagles sailed toward the Promised Land.

When our choir and orchestra performed at Tel Noff, Ayellet Hasahar, and the Jewish Theater in Jerusalem, the performance was electrifying. I could feel the brush of angels' wings and the very presence of God.

What began as a onetime event has now become an annual celebration at Cornerstone Church. Each year in the month of May we televise via satellite "A Night to Honor Israel" from the sanctuary of Cornerstone Church to our national television audience. Sixteen years have passed since September 10, 1981, but the issues are no less pressing today. The personal threats haven't subsided, and the message hasn't been restrained. Verbalized suspicion from both Christians and Jews has never ceased. We don't honor Israel and the Jewish people for applause or approval; we do it because we have a biblical mandate to bless God's people.

Why is the world so quick to turn against Israel? Why has Christianity persecuted the Jews for 2,000 years? How logical is it for Christians to praise dead Jews of the past—Abraham, Isaac, Jacob, David, Jesus, and Paul—while cursing the Jewish people of the present?

The attacks against Israel, against Jerusalem, and eventually against the Jews themselves will escalate toward Jerusalem's darkest hour. The present peace process will prove to be the womb of war. As the fanatical attacks on Jerusalem increase, we must let the world know that if a line has to be drawn, it will be drawn around Christians as well as Jews. We are united and indivisible.

Israel, you are not alone.

CHAPTER 2

HE WHO BLESSES ISRAEL . . .

Israel and its Holy City, Jerusalem, hold the keys to the future. What happens in the Jewish state affects what God is doing with the rest of the world, so the better we understand Israel, the more comprehensive will be our grasp of things to come.

Using a favorite Hebrew figure of speech, Zechariah described Israel as "the apple of God's eye." "For thus says the LORD of hosts," the prophet wrote, "'He sent Me after glory, to the nations which plunder you; for he who touches you touches the apple of His eye'" (Zech. 2:8).

In biological terms, the "apple" is the pupil, or center, of the eye. This is the most sensitive part of the human body. God is saying through the prophet Zechariah, "When you touch Israel, you have touched the most sensitive part of My being. When you attack Israel or the Jewish people, you are sticking your finger in the center of My eye. Do it and see what happens!" Anyone who harms the Jewish people with malice aforethought will experience the instant wrath of God.

Israel's Birthright

God watches over Israel as a protective parent hovers over an only child. In order to understand how those who bless Israel will be blessed themselves, we need to comprehend these four principles:

1. *The nation of Israel was created by a sovereign act of God.* All other nations were created by an act of war or a declaration of men, but Israel was intentionally created by God so that He would have a physical place of inheritance on the earth (Isa. 19:25).

   By what right? By the right of ownership. God created the earth (Gen. 1:1), and it is His to give to whomever He chooses (Ex. 19:5). He chose to give a specific part of the earth to Abraham, Isaac, Jacob, and their descendants, and He sealed His agreement in a blood covenant that He has sworn to uphold forever (Gen. 15:18–21).

2. *God established Israel's national geographic boundaries.* The exact borders of Israel are detailed in Scripture just as our heavenly Father dictated them. The divine Surveyor drove the original stakes into Judean soil and decreed that no one should ever change these property lines. The real estate contract and land covenants were signed in blood and stand to this very hour. Jews have the absolute right as mandated by God to the land of Israel and, more specifically, to the city of Jerusalem.

3. *Israel has a Spy in the sky.* The psalmist wrote that "He who keeps Israel / Shall neither slumber nor sleep" (Ps. 121:4). No nation in the world can match the defensive force guarding the State of Israel. The archangel Michael has a special assignment to guard Israel (see Dan. 10:13, 21; 12:1; Rev. 12:7), and his supernatural power is far greater than all the military muscle of every

army on earth. The Lord stands watch in the darkest night with an eye trained on the nation of Israel and, more specifically, Jerusalem. Those who fight with Israel fight with Him.

4. *Prosperity or punishment depends on how we treat Israel.* In the moment that God covenanted with Abraham, the Almighty gave him an awesome promise: "I will bless those who bless you, / And I will curse him who curses you; / And in you all the families of the earth shall be blessed" (Gen. 12:3). No pronouncement of Scripture is clearer or more decisive. God smiles on the friends of the descendants of Abraham, and they enjoy heavenly favor.

In contrast, God will answer every act of anti-Semitism with harsh and final judgment. This fourth principle is critical for every citizen of the United States of America. No matter how clever our economic policies or how comprehensive our military preparation, the most significant action our nation can take is our compassionate support of the State of Israel. The quickest and most effective way to be on God's side is to stand with the State of Israel and the Jewish people in their hour of need.

A Guideline for Greatness

God blesses the man or nation that blesses Israel or the Jewish people. This principle is demonstrated in the story of Jacob and Laban in Genesis 29–31. Jacob had agreed to work seven years for Laban on the condition that he be given the hand of beautiful Rachel in marriage. Laban deceived Jacob and gave him his homely daughter, Leah, instead, and Jacob was forced to work another seven years for Rachel's hand.

While Jacob worked for Laban, God greatly blessed the deceptive Gentile. When Jacob asked Laban's permission to leave after fourteen years of service, Laban replied, "Please stay, if I have found favor in your eyes, for I have learned by experience that the LORD has blessed me for your sake" (Gen. 30:27). God blessed Laban, a Gentile, through Jacob.

The story of Joseph is another good illustration of how God blesses Gentiles who bless the Jews. Joseph was a Jewish teenager sold into the land of Egypt by his jealous brothers. In time, with his God-given wisdom, Joseph rose from the penitentiary to the pinnacle of power, becoming prime minister of all Egypt. Through a series of dreams, God revealed to Joseph that seven years of plenty would be followed by seven years of worldwide famine. Pharaoh rewarded Joseph's discernment by placing his signet ring on Joseph's hand and a gold chain about his neck. Pharaoh made Joseph, a Jewish slave, the second most powerful man on earth.

Joseph prepared Egypt for the devastating famine by storing grain during the seven years of abundance. When the seven years of famine came, Egypt was at the apex of its power, literally controlling the world's economy through food.

How did this happen? One Jewish man with supernatural revelation literally saved the Gentile world from starvation. God blesses the Gentiles through the Jewish people.

Jesus Himself said, "Salvation is of the Jews" (John 4:22). He was alluding to the Jewish contribution to Christianity, for without Jews, there would be no Christianity. The prophets, the patriarchs, the apostles, the men who wrote the Bible (with the exception of Luke, who was probably Greek), Mary, Joseph, and Jesus—all were Jewish.

In the seventh chapter of Luke, we read of a Roman centurion who had heard of Jesus Christ, the healing Rabbi. He wanted Jesus to come to his house to pray for a sick servant, but it was forbidden for a righteous Jew to enter a Gentile's house. The centurion asked the Jewish elders how he could get Jesus to come and pray for his servant.

What logic did the Jewish elders use to persuade Jesus to help the centurion? They said, "He loves our nation, and has built us a synagogue" (Luke 7:5). This centurion had blessed Israel and the Jewish people with a practical act of kindness, so Jesus prayed for the centurion's servant, who was healed.

In the tenth chapter of Acts the Bible declares that Cornelius, a Roman centurion who lived in Caesarea, gave alms to the Jewish people and was of good reputation among all the nation of the Jews. Cornelius was a righteous man who benefited from the principle of blessing the Jews. What was his most extraordinary blessing?

God gave the apostle Peter a vision of a prayer shawl held by its four corners descending from heaven. All manner of four-footed beasts and wild beasts and creeping things and fowls of the air moved inside this shawl. This vision signified the religious barrier forbidding Jews from associating with unclean Gentiles in spiritual matters. Understanding God's message, Peter went at once to Cornelius's house, preached the gospel, and those in the house were saved and filled with the Spirit.

"While Peter was still speaking these words, the Holy Spirit fell upon all those who heard the word. And those of the circumcision who believed were astonished, as many as came with Peter, because the gift of the Holy Spirit had been poured out on the Gentiles also. For they heard them speak with tongues and magnify God" (Acts 10:44–46).

What made this possible? A Roman centurion—a Gentile—blessed the Jewish people, and God opened the windows of heaven and poured upon him and his house a blessing he could not contain.

American History and Jewish Blessing

Jewish influence has permeated all corners of the globe and every page of history, including American history. Jews were very involved in Columbus's expedition to find the New World. Levi Ben Gershon, a Jew, invented the sea quadrant, used for navigation. Jewish cartographers drew most of the sea charts of the age. And centuries before Columbus, Jews had disproved the notion that the world was flat. In the *Zohar*, 200 years before Columbus, Moses de Leon, a Jew, stated that the earth revolves like a ball and is covered by daylight on one side and darkness on the other.[1]

Jewish influence extended far beyond the discovery of America. During a particularly dark time of the American Revolution, George Washington and the Continental Army were freezing and starving in the snows of Valley Forge. Without food, arms, or ammunition, it seemed that the fledgling nation was doomed to die. But Haym Salomon, a Jewish banker from Philadelphia, arranged for the Jews of the thirteen colonies to respond with financial aid that turned the tide of the war and enabled General Washington to defeat the British. Salomon believed that until Jerusalem would once again welcome the children of Israel, America could be the Promised Land for the Jews.[2]

"It can be documented," writes David Allen Lewis, "that Salomon gave his personal fortune, and in addition raised huge sums of money through business transactions, buying financial papers and leverage accounts on various European and American markets. He could have made himself rich and left a fine estate for his lovely wife and children. He died sick and penniless at the age of 45. . . . He had given all he had, and now his body lies in a lonely, unmarked, forgotten grave in Philadelphia."[3]

No one is certain exactly how much money Haym Salomon loaned to our infant country, but reports range from $600,000 to $800,000. If we assume the loan amount was $700,000, compounded quarterly at 7 percent interest over a period of 222 years, conservative estimates indicate that the United States owes *over $2.5 trillion* to Haym Salomon's heirs. America's foreign aid to Israel doesn't come close to paying our debt to the Jewish people.

Washington was so appreciative of the Jewish contribution to the birth of America that he instructed the engravers of the American one-dollar bill to engrave a tribute to the Jewish people over the head of the bald eagle. If you look carefully, above the eagle's head you'll see the Star of David surrounded by the brilliant light of the Shekinah glory that dwelled above the Mercy Seat in the Holy of Holies in the Jewish tabernacle.[4]

If you turn your one-dollar bill upside down and place your thumb over the eagle's head, the shield becomes the menorah, or the seven golden candlesticks of Israel. Placing your thumb completely over the shield leaves the tail of nine feathers that represent the flames of the Hanukkah Menorah.

But the symbolism doesn't stop there. To the Israelites, the number thirteen was a significant number. Including the Levites, there were thirteen tribes of Israel. Thirteen is also the age at which a boy or girl reaches adulthood. Now look on the one-dollar bill—there are thirteen leaves in the olive branch in the right talon of the eagle, thirteen arrows in the left talon, thirteen stripes on the shield, thirteen stars in the cloud representing the thirteen colonies. Every American who carries a single dollar bill holds a constant reminder that in Israel, "all the nations of the earth shall be blessed."

John Adams, another of our country's founding fathers, respected the Jews. In a letter to his friend F. A. Van der Kemp, he wrote:

> In spite of . . . Voltaire [an ardent anti-Semite], I will insist that the Hebrews have done more to civilize men than any other nation. If I were an atheist and believed in blind eternal fate, I should still believe that fate had ordained the Jews to be the most essential instrument for civilizing the nations. . . . I should believe that chance had ordered the Jews to preserve and to propagate to all mankind the doctrine of a supreme, intelligent, wise, almighty sovereign of the universe, which I believe to be the great essential principle of all morality, and consequently of all civilization.[5]

Pro-Jewish Voices

Sir Winston Churchill

Sir Winston Leonard Spencer Churchill, beloved British statesman, soldier, and author, certainly seemed to enjoy the blessing of God upon his life. He was not only intelligent, but intuitive, and was among the first to publicly issue warnings about the threat of Nazi Germany. Unfortunately, his warnings were not heeded.

In 1940, seven months after the outbreak of World War II, Churchill became Britain's prime minister. His stirring speeches, his energy, and his refusal to placate Hitler were crucial to bolstering the British troops and ensuring that country's resistance to the enemy. In June 1941, after the Germans invaded Russia, Churchill went on British radio and scathingly remarked that when Hitler entered his newly conquered territory, "All his usual formalities of perfidy were observed with scrupulous technique."[6]

Churchill was knighted in 1953, and in that same year was also awarded the Nobel Prize in literature for his writing.[7]

Why did God bless Winston Churchill? I believe it was, in part, because Churchill loved the apple of God's eye, the Jews.

As early as 1908, a full forty years before the State of Israel was established, Churchill expressed his "full sympathy with the historical aspirations of the Jews" to restore "a center of racial and political integrity" in Palestine.[8]

In June 1954 Churchill told a group of American journalists, "I am a Zionist, let me make that clear. I was one of the original ones after the Balfour Declaration and I have worked faithfully for it. I think it is a most wonderful thing that this community should have established itself so effectively, turning the desert into fertile gardens and thriving townships and should have afforded refuge to millions of their co-religionists who suffered so fearfully under Hitler, and not only under Hitler, persecution. I think it is a wonderful thing." He opposed the White Paper Policies that limited the number of Jews who could enter Britain during Hitler's reign of terror, and on the fate of Jerusalem, Churchill had one terse comment—"You ought to let the Jews have Jerusalem; it is they who made it famous."[9]

Chaim Weizmann

During World War I, when the prospect of an Allied victory was dim and freedom in the Western world hung by a thread, the British navy ran short of gunpowder. The First Lord of the Admiralty, Sir Winston Churchill, contacted a brilliant Jewish chemist, Chaim Weizmann, for help. Churchill asked Weizmann if he could produce 30,000 tons of synthetic acetone so the British could manufacture cordite gunpowder. Harnessing his genius and setting his energies to the task, Weizmann produced the synthetic acetone, thus assuring British superiority on the high seas.

When asked what he wanted for his services to England and the Allies, Weizmann replied, "There is only one thing I want—a national homeland for my people." On November 2, 1917, British Foreign Secretary Arthur J. Balfour issued the Balfour Declaration, promising the Jews of the world a homeland. The declaration stated that the British government favored "the establishment in Palestine of a national home for the Jewish people and will use their best endeavours to facilitate the achievement of that object, it being clearly understood that nothing shall be done which may prejudice the civil and religious rights of existing non-Jewish communities in Palestine."[10]

Weizmann saw his dream come true, and in 1948 he was named the first president of Israel. The free world owes a tremendous debt of gratitude to him.

Theodore Roosevelt

Theodore Roosevelt, America's original Rough Rider, had a wry sense of humor, and never was it better displayed than on one occasion when he dealt with an anti-Semite. Roosevelt was police commissioner of New York City in

1895, and an anti-Semitic preacher from Berlin came to New York to preach a crusade against the Jews. "Many of the New York Jews were much excited and asked me to prevent him from speaking and not to give him police protection," Roosevelt wrote in his autobiography. "This, I told them, was impossible; and if possible would have been undesirable because it would have made him a martyr. The proper thing to do was to make him ridiculous.

"Accordingly I detailed for his protection a [Jewish] sergeant and a score or two of [Jewish] policemen. He made his harangue against the Jews under the active protection of some forty policemen, every one of them a Jew."[11]

Albert Einstein

When the Axis powers plunged the world into World War II, again it was the Seed of Abraham to whom God chose to reveal the secrets of the universe. Albert Einstein, an American theoretical physicist, was born a German Jew; he was later recognized as one of the greatest physicists of all time. In 1914 he became titular professor of physics and director of theoretical physics at the Kaiser Wilhelm Institute in Berlin. But under Hitler's anti-Semitic policies, in 1934 the Nazi government confiscated his property and revoked his German citizenship. In 1940 Einstein became an American citizen, holding a post at the Institute for Advanced Study in Princeton from 1933 until his death.

Einstein, the genius who gave the world the formula $E=mc^2$, was well acquainted with anti-Semitism. "If my theory of relativity is proven correct," he said, thinking of his heritage, "Germany will claim me as a German and France will declare that I am a citizen of the world. Should my theory prove untrue, France will say that I am a German and Germany will declare that I am a Jew."[12]

In 1939, when approached by his friend Szilard about new research into atomic power, Einstein sent the following message to President Franklin Delano Roosevelt, urging him to investigate the possible use of atomic energy in bombs:

> Some recent work by E. Fermi and L. Szilard which has been communicated to me in manuscript leads me to expect that the element uranium may be turned into a new and important source of energy in the near future. Certain aspects of the situation which has arisen seem to call for watchfulness and, if necessary, quick action on the part of the Administration. . . . In the course of the last four months it has been made almost certain . . . that it may become possible to set up a nuclear chain reaction in a large mass of uranium, by which vast amounts of power and large quantities of radium-like elements would be generated. . . . This new phenomenon would lead also to the construction of bombs.[13]

Though as an ardent pacifist Einstein was opposed to the use of the atomic bomb, it was as a result of his work that President Harry Truman decided to use the A-bomb. Knowing that the Japanese military leaders were prepared to fight a conventional war to the last man, Truman felt he had no other choice. His decision saved thousands of American lives and brought a halt to World War II.

Other Pro-Jewish Voices

As virulent and prevalent as anti-Semitism is, people throughout history have been willing to take a stand for the Jewish people. Who can forget the example of Corrie ten Boom and her family, who risked their own lives hiding Jews in their homes in Holland? Corrie and her family were sent to the Nazi concentration camps for hiding

Jewish refugees. Her father and sister literally starved to death in the camps. Corrie was released by clerical error and allowed to return to her home in Holland. A tree now grows in her honor in the Avenue of the Righteous Gentiles, just outside the Yad Vashem Centre in Jerusalem.

In 1894, when French intelligence learned that a French soldier had sold military secrets to Germany, Captain Alfred Dreyfus, a Jew, was immediately accused of being the spy. A military tribunal sentenced him to life imprisonment on Devil's Island though all the evidence pointed to the guilt of another soldier, Colonel Marie-Charles-Ferdinand-Walsin Esterhazy.

Fortunately, a few valiant souls would not allow such unfairness to go unchallenged. Émile Zola, a novelist, refused to let the case die. He wrote, "May all my words perish if Dreyfus is not innocent. . . . I did not want my country to remain in lies and injustice. One day, France will thank me for having helped to save its honor."[14]

France did. Despite relentless opposition from the French army, government officials, and the Catholic church, Dreyfus's case was reopened and the man exonerated—twelve years after his arrest.[15]

Changing Attitudes

"After centuries of intolerance, flecked with murder and crude social bigotry," writes David Aikman, "increasing numbers of Christians in recent years have been owning up to the Church's historical role in anti-Semitism. And they have, quite rightly, been repenting of it."[16]

Aikman, a correspondent with *Time* magazine, has noticed that recently many Christians have begun to experience a love for the Jewish people.

At the same time, enamored with Israel and the possibility that the "last days" might be just around the corner, increasing numbers of Christians began to see Jews in general—not just Israelis—no longer as "Christ killers" but as a people chosen by God and beloved by Him no less today than in Old Testament times. Not all Jews have been comfortable with this rather striking change in Christian perceptions of them—from "enemy" to "instrument" of God's purpose, so to speak. After all, some must wonder, if theology was the reason for the original antipathy of Christians toward them, and theology has now given birth to admiration, what happens if theology shifts once again?[17]

Anti-Semitism is sin, and sin damns the soul!

Pope John XXIII, who died in 1963, delivered the most open apology the Jews have ever received from the Catholic church. Shortly before his death, he published this prayer:

> We realize now that many, many centuries of blindness have dimmed our eyes, so that we no longer see the beauty of Thy Chosen People and no longer recognize in their faces the features of our first-born brother. We realize that our brows are branded with the mark of Cain. Centuries long has Abel lain in blood and tears, because we have forgotten Thy love. Forgive us the curse which we unjustly laid on the name of the Jews. Forgive us, that with our curse, we crucified Thee a second time.[18]

Jewish Blessings for All Mankind

There is no denying that mankind has been blessed by the Jewish people. Casimir Funk discovered vitamins;

Abraham Jacobi, founder of American pediatrics, invented the laryngoscope. Jonas Salk developed the polio vaccine. The American Medical Association was founded by a Jewish ophthalmologist, Isaac Hayes. Joseph Goldberger laid the foundation for the science of nutrition, while Simon Baruch was the first physician to identify and successfully complete an appendectomy.[19]

One Jewish man, Emile Berliner, invented the microphone and the gramophone. Other Jews invented calculators, synthetic rubber, and petroleum.

How many times have you enjoyed the works of Jewish people and not even realized it? Consider the many Jews who enrich our lives through entertainment and news: Douglas Fairbanks, Cary Grant, Kirk Douglas, Paul Newman, Shelley Winters, James Caan, George Segal, Goldie Hawn, Dustin Hoffman, Peter Sellers, Debra Winger, Lauren Bacall, John Houseman, Madeline Kahn, Barbra Streisand, Danny Kaye, Edward G. Robinson, Tony Curtis, Rod Steiger, Tony Randall, Jack Klugman, Hal Linden, Peter Falk, Ed Asner, Lorne Greene, George Burns, Gracie Allen, David Janssen, Jack Benny, Michael Landon, Linda Lavin, Ted Koppel, Howard Cosell, Barbara Walters, Mike Wallace, Larry King, and Ann Landers. These people are a living testimony that "in thee shall all the nations of the earth be blessed."

The world has been blessed by God's people, and it is time for us to bless the Jews. We can begin by praying for the nation of Israel and supporting their right to hold Jerusalem in peace. "Pray for the peace of Jerusalem," wrote the psalmist, "May they prosper who love you" (Ps. 122:6). God clearly promises to bless the man, the church, or the nation that blesses the State of Israel or the Jewish people.

From the time of Joseph in Egypt to Einstein in America, God has placed Jewish people at the major intersections of history to bless the world. And I've got news for you—God isn't finished. The people of Israel and their Holy City will soon fill the major role in a coming world drama.

CHAPTER 3

HE WHO
CURSES ISRAEL . . .

The man or nation that lifts a voice or hand against Israel invites the wrath of God. The second half of God's promise to Abraham includes the words, "And I will curse him who curses you" (Gen. 12:3).

History will validate this truth: What you do or attempt to do to the Jewish people, God will do to you.

Egypt

Consider Egypt. This fertile black land produced a wealth that was the envy of the world. The Egyptians built pyramids we study and admire to this day, but the pharaoh of the Exodus enslaved and burdened the children of Abraham, drowning their sons and attempting to crush their spirits with hard labor.

God sent Moses as a deliverer. As the Hebrews crossed the Red Sea, God drowned the sons of the Egyptians en masse as they pursued the Jews. In the end, Pharaoh's mighty army was consumed by God's wrath as He drowned them in the Red Sea. Pharaoh himself was soon found floating faceup, grotesquely bloated in the heat of Egypt's sun, his sightless eyes staring at God, whom he could not see and would never know. His arrogant query, "Who is the Lord, that I should obey Him?" received a divine response. In one hour, the most powerful man on earth was reduced to fish food!

Exactly what Egypt did to Israel, God did to Egypt.

Amalekites

Consider the Amalekites. As the children of Israel came out of the wilderness, the people of Amalek fought with Israel in a place called Rephidim (Ex. 17:8). Their objective was to utterly destroy Israel. God responded with rage. He said to Moses, "Write this for a memorial in the book and recount it in the hearing of Joshua, that I will utterly blot out the remembrance of Amalek from under heaven. And Moses built an altar and called its name, The-LORD-Is-My-Banner; for he said, 'Because the LORD has sworn: the LORD will have war with Amalek from generation to generation'" (Ex. 17:14–16).

What happened to the Amalekites? Seven hundred years later, when Saul was king of Israel, God sent Samuel to the king with this message: "Thus says the LORD of hosts: 'I will punish Amalek for what he did to Israel, how he ambushed him on the way when he came up from Egypt. Now go and attack Amalek, and utterly destroy all that they have, and do not spare them. But kill both man and woman, infant and nursing child, ox and sheep, camel and donkey'" (1 Sam. 15:2–3). Exactly what the Amalekites tried to do to Israel, God did to the Amalekites.

Haman

Consider Haman, the Old Testament Hitler who, in the book of Esther, devised a plan to exterminate the Jews of Persia. At that point in history, most of the Jews of the world were living under Persian control. Haman's success would have produced a holocaust that would have prevented the Word of God from being written by Jewish authors *and* Jesus Christ from being born. Haman planned to hang Mordecai, the Jew he hated most. But Haman and his sons were hanged on the very gallows he had designed for the Seed of Abraham. Exactly what Haman planned for the Jews, God did to Haman.

Spain

Consider Spain. In the midst of its so-called Golden Era, Spain was a world power in the fourteenth century. More than 850,000 Jews lived in that country, and they were valuable members of society who made great contributions. But in 1492, as Queen Isabella sought to purify the aristocracy, the Spanish crown issued an Edict of Expulsion. All Jews who were willing to convert could remain in Spain, all others were forced, upon pain of death, to leave immediately.

The Seed of Abraham left Spain at the same time Columbus sailed across the Atlantic and discovered the New World that would become another haven for the Jews. Spain slipped into the graveyard of human history as its Golden Era ended. Spain learned what Egypt and the Amalekites had learned.

John Phillips states that "not until the coming of Hitler did the Jews suffer such widespread persecution as they did in Spain. The decline and fall of the Spanish Empire can be dated from the time that Spain expelled all its Jews."[1]

England

Consider England. England has vacillated in its treatment of the Jews. At one time every Jew in England, regardless of age or sex, was imprisoned, and all Jewish wealth was confiscated. Another time they were expelled from England and not allowed to return for 400 years.

In more recent history, consider the British publication of the infamous White Paper Policy that barred the Jews of the Holocaust from entering Israel. By force the British captured Jews who had gone to Israel to escape Hitler and the Nazi death camps. After capturing them, the British sent them back to Europe to die.

With limited arms and an indefatigable spirit, the Jews of Palestine vigorously fought the British to prevent the certain death of fellow Jews. The Irgun, a Jewish resistance group brilliantly led by Menachem Begin, fought the British in battles that led to a stalemate.

In 1947 Great Britain's ambassador to the United Nations voted against Israel becoming a state. When Israel achieved statehood despite the British veto, British officers led the Arab armies in an all-out military attack, trying to exterminate the State of Israel at its birth.

Depending on its treatment of the Jews, the influence and prestige of Great Britain have waxed and waned. The kingdom that once boasted the "sun would never set on its dominions" is now a very small kingdom indeed.

Adolf Hitler

Consider Adolf Hitler. As a spiritual leader in the Roman Catholic Church, Hitler made the following outrageous statements about the Jews:

- "In the heart of every Jew flows a traitor's blood."
- "A Jewish child over the age of seven can be baptized against its parents' will."
- "No Christian may be in the service of a Jew."
- "No Christian woman may nurse a Jewish infant; this would appear to the Church an outrage; it means bringing the devil into contact with the Holy Ghost." (In Hitler's view, of course, the devil was the Jewish infant.)
- "A Christian may not eat with a Jew."
- "Even in a prayer the Jew must be referred to as 'perfidious.'"
- "A Jew may not be a soldier; he may only be a clothes dealer, a ragman, a peddler, or a money lender."[2]

I'm sure you don't need me to remind you of Hitler's evil. Over six million innocent Jews perished at his hands, and what was his end? He shot himself and ordered his fanatical followers to burn his body in order to prevent the Russians from mocking him as Mussolini was mocked after death.

Hitler closed his eyes in death and stepped into eternity to meet a Rabbi named Jesus of Nazareth as his final judge. "I will curse him who curses you. . . ."

Stalin and the Jews

In his book *Exploring the World of the Jew*, John Phillips recounts the fascinating story of Russia's Joseph Stalin and the Jews. When Stalin came to power, he never forgot that his greatest rival had been Leon Trotsky, a Jew born Lev Davidovich Bronstein. During Stalin's reign of terror, no prominent Jew was ever safe from persecution.

In early 1953 Stalin's secret police arrested nine "terrorist doctors," six of whom were Jewish, and charged them with plotting to murder Soviet leaders. The plot was a total fabrication, but Stalin laid careful plans to use this ridiculous story to proceed with his goals for the extermination of all Russian Jews.

Stalin read a statement to the assembled politburo outlining his plan of extermination. The Russian doctors would be tried, then hanged in Moscow. This would be followed by three days of "spontaneous rioting" against the Jews. The government would then step in and separate the Jews from the Russian people and ship the Jews to Siberia. Two-thirds of the captives, however, would never arrive—the "angry Russian people" would kill them along the way. The third who did arrive would die swiftly in slave labor camps.

Stalin's proposal was met with stunned silence. His plans proceeded, and the nine doctors were only days away from their execution when Stalin suffered a stroke on March 5.

On April 3, *Pravda* announced that the nine doctors had been declared "not guilty" and released. I have to agree with John Phillips's statement about this situation: "There is sometimes a grim appropriateness about the timing of God."[3] God watches over the apple of His eye.

Contemporary Evidence of God's Justice

Adolf Hitler systematically murdered six million Jews because good men did nothing and said nothing in the day of trouble.

In 1985, when I stood at Checkpoint Charlie and looked at the Berlin Wall, the young German woman the military had assigned as my personal guide asked, "Pastor Hagee, why did God allow the Communists to build a wall around the German people?"

My answer jolted her out of her shoes. "God allowed the Communists to build a wall around the Germans because your parents built a wall around the Jews," I told her. "What you do to the Jewish people, God will do to you."

As she gasped in surprise, I pointed to the fence dividing East and West Berlin. "Look at that fence," I said. "It's the same height as the fence at Dachau. It's electrified just like the fence at Dachau. It has guard towers in the center with attack dogs trained to rip out your throat—just like Dachau. God has done to you what you did to the Jews!"

Why should America support Israel? Because the blessing of God depends upon it. We do not have to agree with every political position Israel takes, but if we, as a nation, make Israel's life grievous by design, we will face the wrath of God.

The Jews' Divine Preservation

Mark Twain wrote the following in September 1898:

> If the statistics are right, the Jews constitute but one percent of the human race. It suggests a nebulous dim

puff of star dust lost in the blaze of the Milky Way. Properly the Jew ought hardly to be heard of; but he is heard of. He is as prominent on the planet as any other people, and his commercial importance is extravagantly out of proportion to the smallness of his bulk. His contributions to the world's list of great names in literature, science, art, music, finance, medicine, and abstruse learning are also away out of proportion to the weakness of his numbers. . . . The Egyptian, the Babylonian, and the Persian rose, filled the planet with sound and splendor, then faded to dreamstuff and passed away; the Greek and the Roman followed, and made a fast noise, and they are gone; other peoples have sprung up and held their torch high for a time, but it burned out, and they sit in twilight now, or have vanished. The Jew saw them all, beat them all, and is now what he always was, exhibiting no decadence, no infirmities of age, no weakening of his parts, no slowing of his energies, no dulling of his alert and aggressive mind. All things are mortal but the Jew; all other forces pass, but he remains. What is the secret of his immortality?[4]

I can explain the secret in just seven words: Israel is the apple of God's eye!

Where are the ancient civilizations today? Gone with the wind. They are little more than historical footnotes recognized by scholars and librarians. Where are the Jews? They flourish in Israel and around the globe. Why? Because He that keeps Israel never slumbers or sleeps. He keeps watch over His beloved ones.

The Battle for Jerusalem

The battle for Israel is now on the agenda of the National Council of Churches. In my office I have a copy of a one-page ad placed in *The New York Times* by the NCC.[5] In the name of peace, the ad calls for a "shared Jerusalem."

A shared Jerusalem? Never! A "shared Jerusalem" means control of the Holy City would be wrested away from the Jewish people and given, at least in part, to the Palestine Liberation Organization. I say "never," not because I dislike Arab people or Palestinians, but because the Word of God says it is God's will for Jerusalem to be under the exclusive control of the Jewish people until Messiah comes. According to Genesis chapters 12, 13, 15, 17, 26, and 28, only the Jewish people have a legitimate claim to the city. That's not my viewpoint, that's God's opinion! God doesn't care what the United Nations thinks or what the NCC believes. He gave Jerusalem to the nation of Israel, and it is theirs.

As Christian friends of Israel, we must urge the United States government to continue its unshakable support for the State of Israel and the Jewish people as the only legitimate heirs to the city of Jerusalem. Isaiah 62:6–7 urges us: "You who make mention of the LORD, do not keep silent, / And give Him no rest till He establishes / And till He makes Jerusalem a praise in the earth."

If we can learn anything from the example of those who cursed Israel, it is this: If America turns its back in Israel's hour of need, Israel will survive—but America will not. God could crush this nation economically by sending a depression that will make the crash of 1929 look like a walk in the park.

If we want to experience the unlimited favor of God, if we want to experience an explosion of prosperity, if we want a fresh outpouring of the Holy Spirit, we must bless Israel and oppose those who would curse the apple of God's eye.

Chapter 4

The Crucifixion of the Jews

Of all the bigotries that savage the human temper there is none so stupid as [anti-Semitism]. In the sight of these fanatics, Jews . . . can do nothing right.

If they are rich, they are birds of prey. If they are poor, they are vermin.

If they are in favor of war, that is because they want to exploit the bloody feuds of Gentiles to their own profit. If they are anxious for peace they are either instinctive cowards or traitors.

If they give generously—and there are no more liberal givers than the Jews—they are doing it for some selfish purpose of their own. If they don't give, then what would one expect of a Jew?[1]

—David Lloyd George, British prime minister

The Jewish people have been persecuted throughout history. They were enslaved in Egypt, deported by the Assyrians, attacked by Nebuchadnezzar, nearly purged by Haman, and oppressed by Roman rule. The crucifixion of the Jews began with the pulpit propaganda of the early church fathers: Eusebius of Caesarea, Cyril, Chrysostom, Augustine, Origen, Justin, and Jerome. These men carried out an orchestrated and enormous campaign against the Jews, portraying them as "killers of Christ, plague carriers, demons, children of the devil, bloodthirsty pagans who are as deceitful as Judas was relentless."

The church fathers spelled the traitor's name as *Jewdas*. As Pope Gelasius I (A.D. 492–96) philosophized: "In the Bible the whole is often named after the part; as Judas was called a devil and the devil's workman, he gives his name to the whole race."[2]

How can we forget that Jesus was a Jew? That the apostles were Jewish? In condemning "the whole race," the church fathers condemned the apostles and the Savior they worshiped!

Desiderius Erasmus, an ordained Roman Catholic priest and one of the leading figures of the Renaissance, once stated, "If to hate Jews is to be a good Christian, we are all good Christians."[3]

Sometimes the Jews were hated for no good reason. One particular story about the Roman emperor Hadrian illustrates the depth of his hatred for the Jews. It is said that a Jew passed in front of Hadrian and greeted him. The emperor asked, "Who are you?"

The man answered, "I am a Jew."

"How dare a Jew pass in front of Hadrian and greet him?" the emperor roared. "Off with his head!"

Moments later, another Jew, who had not seen this exchange, passed in front of the emperor and did *not* greet him. Hadrian called out and asked, "Who are you?"

The man answered, "I am a Jew."

"How dare a Jew pass in front of Hadrian without giving a greeting?" he stormed. "Off with his head!"

Hadrian's senators said, "We don't understand your actions. How can you put to death the man who greeted you as well as the man who did not greet you?"

Hadrian scornfully replied: "Do you dare to advise me how I am to deal with those I hate?"[4]

The Jewish people were portrayed by the church fathers as bloodthirsty torturers of the Savior, pitiless killers, traitors who sold their souls for thirty pieces of silver, money changers who desecrated the temple, and more cruel than beasts because they demanded that the legs of the dying Christ be broken. In short, early church fathers taught that Jews were sons of the devil.

The church's earliest historian, Eusebius of Caesarea, declared his intention in *Church History* "to recount the misfortunes which immediately came upon the whole Jewish nation in consequence of their plots against the Savior."[5]

Eusebius only set the stage for his contemporaries. Saint Gregory of Nyssa mounted his pulpit ranting about the Jews:

> Slayers of the Lord, murderers of the prophets, adversaries of God, haters of God, men who show contempt for the law, foes of grace, enemies of their fathers' faith, advocates of the devil, brood of vipers, slanderers, scoffers, men whose minds are in darkness, leaven of the Pharisees, assembly of demons, sinners, wicked men, stoners and haters of righteousness.[6]

The Golden Mouth

The venom of Christian hatred for the Jews reached its crescendo with the coming of Saint John Chrysostom (A.D.

345–407), known as the "bishop with the golden mouth." One of the first to describe the Jews as "killers of Christ," for centuries Chrysostom's anti-Semitic venom was considered classic Roman church reading.

"How can Christians," he wrote, "dare have the slightest converse with Jews, the most miserable of all men?"[7] He went on to write:

> The Jews are the most worthless of all men. They are lecherous, greedy, rapacious. They are perfidious murderers of Christ. They worship the devil, their religion is a sickness. The Jews are the odious assassins of Christ and for killing God there is no expiation possible, no indulgence or pardon. Christians may never cease vengeance, and the Jew must live in servitude forever. God always hated the Jews. It is incumbent upon all Christians to hate the Jews.[8]

Chrysostom wrote that the Jewish synagogue was a "theater and a house of prostitution," a "cavern of brigands," a "repair of wild beasts," and "the domicile of the devil."[9] This Christian wrote that he hated the Jews because of their "odious assassination of Christ."[10] For this, he said, "there is no expiation possible, no indulgence, no pardon. . . . God hates the Jews and always hated the Jews. . . . I hate the Jews also because they outrage the law."[11]

The natural progression for popular hatred is action. Religious belief fosters deep feeling, and deep feeling demands that action be taken to support that basic belief. Christian action toward the Jews exploded with a demonic violence beyond comprehension.

At Easter, when the Christian clergy would inflame the passions of the faithful with the vengeful message that the Jews killed Christ, the congregants would race out of the church toward the Jewish quarter with clubs and beat Jews to death for what they did to Jesus on the cross.[12]

In some churches it became an annual custom at Easter to drag a Jew into the church and slap him on the face before the altar. Malcolm Hay explains:

> This ceremony was sometimes carried out with excessive vigor; on one occasion, recounts a monkish chronicler (without, however, expressing any disapproval), a distinguished nobleman who was taking part as chief celebrant "knocked out the eyes and the brains of the perfidious one (disbelieving Jew), who fell dead on the spot . . . his brethren from the synagogue took the body out of the Church and buried it."[13]

The torrent of hate continued in medieval times.

The Crusades

While some knights undoubtedly fit the romantic and popular notion of a chivalrous warrior on a holy pilgrimage to fight for a godly cause, most Christians are unaware of the tragic truth. The crusaders were, in fact, seasoned soldiers operating under a blanket of papal protection known as the indulgence. In issuing a call for the First Crusade, the Council of Clermont and Pope Urban summarized the benefits for a potential participant. The action the crusaders were about to undertake, they wrote, would be a penance so inclusive that it would pay back to God not only the debts of punishment owed for some past sins, but would also "pay for" sins recently committed.[14] In other words, the crusaders could kill, maim, rape, and steal from the Jews with impunity—and God would turn a blind eye to their sins. Any potential crusader who had been excommunicated from the church would be welcomed back into the fold with full forgiveness.

Not only were the crusaders promised forgiveness of *sin,* they also were promised the forgiveness of *debt.* Any man who answered the call of the Crusade could consider all of his financial debts to any Jewish creditor canceled. As a bonus, Christian crusaders were permitted to rob the Jews on the journey to and from Jerusalem.

During the First Crusade to the Holy Land, the crusading armies left a trail of Jewish blood across Europe. Within a three-month period, 12,000 Jews were slaughtered in Germany as the crusaders screamed, "The Jews have killed our Savior. They must convert or be killed."

Some Jewish communities were given the opportunity to save their lives by meeting the crusaders' demands for gold and silver. Those who could not meet the ransom demands were butchered "by the will of God." Others ran to the synagogue for sanctuary, locked the doors, said a final prayer, and then killed their wives and children quickly, lest the cross-carrying crusaders torture and butcher them. The fathers committed suicide to preserve the sanctity of the name of Jehovah God.

Not all the crusaders went to the Holy Land. Pope Urban II actively urged Catalan nobles who had taken the sign of the cross to fulfill their vows in Spain. In return for aiding the Church of Tarragona, they were given indulgences and promised the forgiveness of sin.[15]

Christians throughout Europe were armed and given an official holy pardon to kill, loot, and destroy anyone they considered an infidel. Immediately, appalling violence was unleashed against the Jews of northern France and the Rhineland, a region along the Rhine River in western Germany. Many of these crusaders, poor warriors who could not afford to mount a campaign to the Holy Land, were exceedingly brutal, vicious, and ferocious.[16] These were not genteel knights schooled in honor and chivalry. These were hungry, brutal, vengeful men intent upon rape and murder.

In the Rhineland city of Worms—a town between Mannheim and Mainz—lies an ancient Jewish cemetery. Some of the graves date from the eleventh century and three days in May 1096 when 800 Jews were massacred by crusaders setting out for the Promised Land.[17]

Crusaders under the command of Count Emich of Leiningren, a leading noble from Swabia, pulled the Jews from their houses, dragged them through the streets, and gave them the option of conversion or death. "Count Emich's fervor as a crusader was in no doubt, but it was hysterical and ignorant," writes Malcolm Billings. "He claimed to have a cross miraculously branded on his flesh, and some of his followers later marched behind a remarkable goose that was supposed to have been imbued with the Holy Spirit."[18]

Emich began to attack Jews near Speyer before he arrived at Worms, and 1,000 Jews fell victim to his campaign of terror in the town of Mainz. "It was not just a spontaneous outburst of greed and hooliganism by a leaderless collection of peasants," writes Billings. "That comforting thought is now dismissed by historians who believe that many nobles and experienced captains from Swabia, the Low Countries, France and England, who had joined Emich's crusade, encouraged the mobs."[19]

Arguing that the Jews were the race responsible for Christ's crucifixion, the nobles demonstrated how the clergy's call to free "Christ's inheritance," or Jerusalem, became distorted in the minds of listeners. One Count, a man called Dithmar, reportedly said he would not leave Germany until he had killed a Jew. "The road to the Holy Land," reports Billings, "ran through what Jews later came to describe as the first Holocaust."[20]

As Godfrey of Bouillon took Jerusalem in the summer of 1099, he and his men spent their first week slaughtering Jews. When more than 900 Jewish women and children ran to their synagogue for safety, the crusaders set it ablaze. As the screams for mercy mingled with the roaring inferno, the crusaders marched around the synagogue singing "Christ, we adore Thee."[21] After taking Communion, the men who carried the cross into Jerusalem heartily devoted the day to exterminating Jewish men, women, and children—killing more than 10,000.[22] In a search for loot and treasure, Christian soldiers killed every man, woman, and child they met. When Raymond of Aguilers walked through the city, he saw "piles of heads, hands and feet . . . in the houses and streets, and indeed there was a running to and fro of men and knights over the corpses."[23]

Unbelievable? Yes, but even more, unconscionable! No wonder the word *crusade* has the power to nauseate some Jews.

Turn to the pages of Sir Walter Scott's great classic *Ivanhoe*. The story's plot is rife with expressions of hate and barbarism as the Christian Knights Templar prepare to burn a Jewish woman at the stake—another example of the prejudice against Jews during medieval times.

In 1208 Pope Innocent III wrote, "The Jews, against whom the blood of Jesus calls out . . . must remain vagabonds upon the earth, until their faces be covered with shame and they seek the name of Jesus Christ the Lord."[24]

And G. K. Chesterton, a twentieth-century Catholic author whose works are used in parochial schools, once expressed his regret that "the Crusaders who slaughtered

Jewish men, women and children could not be canonized [named as saints]."[25]

The Fourth Lateran Council

In November 1215, in response to the call of Pope Innocent III, the Fourth Lateran Council met in Rome. More than 1,000 delegates met in stormy sessions to determine what the official relationship between Christians and Jews should be. The official Christian policy, issued in a formal declaration, supported the conduct of the Roman church for centuries to come.

Concerned that Christians and Jews would intermingle, the Fourth Lateran Council decreed that all Jews must wear a "Jewish badge." Also, "That the crime of such a sinful mixture shall no longer find evasion or cover under pretext of error, we order that the Jews of both sexes, in all Christian lands and at all times, shall be publicly differentiated from the rest of the population by the quality of their garment, especially since this is ordained by Moses."[26]

The reference to Moses refers to the fact that Moses instructed the men of Israel to make prayer shawls (Num. 15:37–41) to be worn by adult men. Jesus Christ wore a prayer shawl from His thirteenth birthday until the day of His crucifixion. Taking this instruction completely out of context, the church fathers used Moses' instruction to force all Jews of both sexes to dress distinctively. When Hitler came to power, he used this long-established policy to force the Jews to wear a yellow Star of David, marking them for abuse and execution.

The Fourth Lateran Council also decreed that Jews could not hold public office. Following the spirit of this edict, on April 7, 1933, the Third Reich passed a law titled "Law for the Restoration of the Professional Civil Service." This lofty-sounding piece of legislation was the legal instrument through which the Nazis dismissed every Jew in Germany working at a civil service job. Overnight, thousands of Jews found themselves without jobs.

Finally, the Fourth Lateran Council ruled that Jews must tithe to the Roman church. Ten percent of any Jew's income was to be paid to the church because the Jews were now owners of lands that had previously belonged to Christians. The edict states: "And under the threat of the same penalty [social and economic boycott] we decree that Jews should be compelled to make good the tithes and dues owed to the Churches which the Churches have been accustomed to receive from the houses and other possessions of the Christians before they came into possession of the Jews, regardless of the circumstances, so that the Church be preserved against loss."[27]

Forcing Jews to tithe was nothing short of extortion, but the church could not afford a loss of revenue. The church was far from finished with the Jews. The church officially endorsed the ghetto system in 1555, in which Jews had to live apart from Christians. Under Pope Clement VIII, the persecution of Jews became a fixed part of papal policy.[28]

The Spanish Inquisition

In 1235 the Council of Arles had introduced a yellow circular patch that Jews were required to wear, and in 1391 massacres of Jews had occurred throughout Spain. Thousands of Jews converted to Christianity in order to avoid massacre, yet the Spaniards remained suspicious of these *conversos*. These people were hated by the Jews for being traitors to Judaism and despised by the church. All attempts to separate the new converts from Judaism via legislation, ghettoization, or education were fruitless.

The Spanish Inquisition struck the Jews like a bolt of lightning out of a blue sky. Queen Isabella and her husband, Ferdinand, were faced with three pressing problems: a political desire to achieve religious conformity in Spain, the failure of pressure to force Jews and Muslims to convert to Christianity, and a profound fear that insincere converts would somehow contaminate the Christian faith.[29] In other words, the Spaniards were afraid of the Jews—particularly since many Jews had intermarried with Spaniards and achieved considerable financial power and social status.

In 1474 Isabella ascended to the throne of Castile, and in 1479 Ferdinand succeeded to that of Aragon. In order to unite these two kingdoms and reassert the predominance of the aristocracy, Isabella and Ferdinand appealed to Pope Sixtus IV to establish an Inquisitor General. Fray Tomás de Torquemada was appointed, and the Inquisition was revived.

The king and queen gave the Jewish population of Spain exactly four months to decide whether they wanted to leave the country or to remain and convert to Christianity. Between 165,000 and 400,000 Jews left Spain before the end of July, many of them abandoning their businesses and paying exorbitant taxes to port officials as they departed. Despite the threat of persecution, as many as 50,000 Jews decided to remain in Spain.[30]

Those who remained faced a nightmare. Under the fanatical leadership of de Torquemada, treatment of the Jews reached levels of torture the world would not see again until Hitler's sadistic Nazi SS Corps blossomed into its fullest level of madness. In the effort to determine who was truly a loyal Christian and who was not, Jewish children were choked to death in the presence of their parents. Women's naked breasts were seared with hot irons to make them betray their husbands. The bodies of men were stretched on the rack where they were pulled in half, forcing them through excruciating pain to denounce their wives and children as false converts.

Published manuals of the Inquisition listed hints on how to spot a "backsliding Jew." Recorded along with these so-called insights were instructions on how to extend and intensify the suffering of the Jewish subject by flame, garrote, rack, whip, and needle. This cruelty, performed in the name of Christ, reached a pinnacle of expertise that left Reinhard Heydrich and Adolf Eichmann little to add for the Third Reich.

Historian Dagobert Runes notes:

> Neither illness nor pregnancy could spare a woman from the bit of the Inquisition instruments wielded by the protectors of the loving Christ. Since all the property of the convicted fell to the Inquisition corporation, to be shared equally by their majesties, there was an added incentive to intensify the Inquisition. Denouncers were well rewarded, and a person denounced was a person indicted and convicted, since no living creature could withstand the refined methods of punishment the clerics had devised. Every single part of the human anatomy had been carefully studied and experimented upon to find those most sensitive to pain.[31]

The Inquisition and its horror continued for years. As late as 1568, a Spanish woman was arrested on the grounds of not eating pork and changing her linen on Saturday. On the testimony of her neighbors, she was arrested and tortured, accused of being Jewish.[32]

The Spanish Inquisition gave birth to the phrase *limpieza de sangre,* meaning "purity of blood." The purity of blood and racial background were major considerations in the trial of an accused Jew. Because the Spaniards were intent upon purifying their aristocracy, those who could not prove that they were of pure Christian descent for at least three generations were doomed to unspeakable torture and death.

Hitler's blood-purity rule, which demanded that Germans prove they had no Jewish ancestors in the three previous generations, was clearly formulated from the example of the church 500 years before Hitler came to power.

Prejudice in the Reformation

"The worst evil genius of Germany," wrote Dean Inge, "is not Hitler, or Bismarck, or Frederick the Great, but Martin Luther." Luther's hatred for the Jews "was intensified by his intellectual vanity and the vigor of his faith, which, like that of many others before and since his time, was united to an equally unshakable conviction that anyone who did not agree with him was an obstinate enemy of the Holy Spirit who deliberately closed his eyes to the truth."[33]

Luther—who at one time wrote of the Jews, "We are aliens and in-laws, they are blood relatives, cousins, and brothers of our Lord"[34]—changed his views when the children of Israel did not convert to his reformed Christianity and join his assault on the Roman church. Luther said of the Jews, "All the blood kindred of Christ burn in Hell, and they are rightly served, even according to their own words they spoke to Pilate."[35]

Moreover, "The only Bible you have any right to," he told the Jews, "is that concealed beneath the sow's tail; the letters that drop from it you are free to eat and drink."[36] What a crude insult to the people of God!

The most vicious, hateful statements Luther ever wrote are found in his tract "On the Jews and Their Lies." In this work he wrote, "Know this, Christian, you have no greater enemy than the Jew." His tract called for the enslavement of the Jews because they were children of the devil and should never touch a Christian's hand. Luther demanded that their synagogues be burned to the ground, their books destroyed, their homes laid waste, their cash and treasure of silver and gold be taken from them, their rabbis be forbidden to teach, and "their tongues be cut out from their throats." He also advised that "young and strong Jews and Jewesses be given the flail, the ax, the hoe, the spade, the distaff, and spindle, and let them earn their bread by the sweat of their noses as is enjoined upon Adam's children. We ought to drive the lazy bones out of our system. . . ."[37]

"If, however," Luther continued, "we are afraid that they might harm us personally, or our wives, children, servants, cattle, etc., then let us apply the same cleverness [expulsion] as the other nations, such as France, Spain, Bohemia, etc., and settle with them for that which they have extorted from us, and after having divided up fairly let us drive them out of the country for all time.

"To sum up, dear princes and nobles who have Jews in your domains, if this advice of mine does not suit you, then find a better one so that you and we may all be free from this insufferable devilish burden—the Jews."[38]

Two days after writing this, Martin Luther died.

When the Nazis placed the Jews in ghetto stables and camps, they were following Luther's precepts. When they burned Jewish synagogues, homes, and schools, they carried out Luther's will. When the Germans robbed the Jews of their possessions, they did Luther's bidding. When the Germans reduced the Jews to concentration camp slavery, they followed Luther's teaching.

Adolf Hitler loved Luther's theology. His Nazi murder machine showed "a proper appreciation of the continuity of their history when they declared that the first large-scale Nazi program, in November, 1938, was a pious operation performed in honor of the anniversary of Luther's birthday."[39]

Twentieth-Century Persecution

Adolf Hitler publicly praised the later teachings of Martin Luther and carried out Luther's recommended attack against the Jews. With the teachings of the early church fathers to support him, Hitler set his plan for genocide into motion. The unwillingness of other countries to offer refuge to Jews convinced Hitler that he had international support for his crusade and that he was doing a good thing.

Roy Eckert has demonstrated how the Nazis prepared the German people for extermination of the Jews by exploiting the crucifixion theme with its corollary of unending divine judgment. The labeling of Jews as "Christ-Killers" motivated the German people to be silent and turn their backs while the Nazis marched Abraham's descendants toward mass extermination camps and finally into the ovens.

In 1942 officials in the Russian army examined Kerch, one of the largest Nazi extermination pits. One of their officers filed this report:

> It was discovered that this trench, one kilometer in length, four meters wide, and two meters deep, was filled to overflowing with bodies of women, children, old men, and boys and girls in their teens. Near the

trench were frozen pools of blood. Children's caps, toys, ribbons, torn off buttons, gloves, milk bottles, and rubber comforters, small shoes, galoshes, together with torn off hands and feet, and other parts of human bodies, were lying nearby. Everything was spattered with blood and brains.[40]

How could this madness happen in one of the most civilized and cultured nations on earth? How could such crimes be justified in the minds of German Christians? These heinous acts were excused with the oft-repeated phrase, "the Jews are the Christ-killers!"

The world's finest scholars have chronicled Hitler's atrocities toward the Jews. There is no purpose in retracing his bloody steps, but I want you to see that church policy shaped the policy of the Third Reich. When Hitler signed the Concordant with the Roman Church, he said, "I am only continuing the work of the Catholic Church."[41]

Let's examine the historical record.

ROMAN CHURCH POLICY	NAZI POLICY
1. Prohibition of intermarriage and of sexual intercourse between Christians and Jews, Synod of Elvira, A.D. 306.	**1.** Law for the Protection of German Blood and Honor, September 15, 1935.
2. Jews and Christians not permitted to eat together, Synod of Elvira, A.D. 306.	**2.** Jews barred from dining cars, December 30, 1939.
3. Jews not allowed to hold public office, Synod of Clermont, A.D. 535. Also Fourth Lateran Council, 1215.	**3.** Law for Re-Establishment of the Professional Civil Service, April 7, 1935, by which Jews were expelled from office and civil service jobs.

4. Jews not allowed to employ Christian servants or possess Christian slaves, Third Synod of Orleans, A.D. 538.

4. Law for the Protection of German Blood and Honor, September 15, 1935, forbade Germans from hiring Jews.

5. Jews not permitted to show themselves in the streets during Passion Week, Third Synod of Orleans, A.D. 538.

5. Decree authorizing local authorities to bar Jews from the streets on certain days (Nazi holidays), December 3, 1938.

6. Burning of the Talmud and other books, Twelfth Synod of Toledo, A.D. 681.

6. Nazi book burnings in Germany.

7. Christians not permitted to patronize Jewish doctors, Trulanic Synod, A.D. 692.

7. Decree of July 25, 1938, forbidding Germans from patronizing Jewish doctors.

8. Jews obligated to pay taxes for support of the church to the same extent as Christians, Fourth Lateran Council, 1215.

8. Jews to pay a special tax in lieu of donations for Party purposes imposed on Nazis, December 24, 1940.

9. Jews not permitted to be plaintiffs or witnesses against Christians in the courts, Third Lateran Council, 1179.

9. Jews not permitted to institute civil suits.

10. Jews not permitted to withhold inheritance from descendants who had accepted Christianity, Third Lateran Council, 1179.

10. Decree empowering the Justice Ministry to void wills offending the "sound judgment of the people," July 31, 1938.

11. Jews must wear a distinctive badge, Fourth Lateran Council, 1215.

11. Decree forcing all Jews to wear the yellow Star of David, September 1, 1941.

12. Construction of new synagogues prohibited, Council of Oxford, 1222.

12. Destruction of synagogues in entire Reich, November 10, 1938. The Jews refer to this night as *Kristalnacht*.

13. Christians not permitted to attend Jewish ceremonies, Synod of Vienna, 1267.

13. Friendly relations with Jews prohibited, October 24, 1941.

14. Jews forced to live in ghettos away from Christians, Synod of Breslau, 1267.

14. Jews forced to live in ghettos, order of Heydrich, September 21, 1939.

15. Jews not permitted to obtain academic degrees, Council of Basel, 1434.

15. All Jews expelled from schools and universities throughout the Third Reich with the Law Against Overcrowding of German Schools and Universities, April 25, 1933.

16. Mass extermination of the Jews in the Crusades. Fourth Lateran Council called upon secular powers to "exterminate all heretics," 1215. The Inquisition burned Jews at the stake while confiscating their property, 1478.

16. Hitler's Final Solution called for the systematic slaughter of every Jew in Europe. He took their homes, their jobs, their possessions (even the gold fillings in their teeth), and finally, their lives. His justification? "It's the will of God and the work of the Church."

The Holocaust did not begin with Hitler lining up the Jews outside the gas chambers. It began with religious leaders sowing the seeds of hatred toward Jews within their congregations. "I am convinced," wrote Pierre van Passen, "that Hitler neither could nor would have done to the Jewish people what he has done . . . if we had not actively prepared the way for him by our own unfriendly attitude to the Jews, by our selfishness and by the anti-Semitic teaching in our churches and schools."[42]

At the Nuremberg trials for major war criminals, a German general was asked how one of the world's most advanced societies could systematically murder six million people. He answered, "I am of the opinion that when for years, for decades, the doctrine is preached that Jews are not even human, such an outcome is inevitable."[43]

Hitler's Testimony

Most Christians have difficulty understanding why Jewish people think of Adolf Hitler as a Christian. Most Jews think Hitler was a Christian for the same reason the Southern Baptists think Billy Graham is a Christian. Billy Graham attended and graduated from a Christian school. He gives dynamic public testimony that he is a Christian in good standing with the Southern Baptist Convention. When he preaches, he quotes the Bible and announces that he is called of God to carry out His mission. Billy Graham's life and ministry verify that he is a man of God.

By no means am I meaning to equate Adolf Hitler with Billy Graham, but consider this: Adolf Hitler attended a Christian school under the tutelage of Padre Bernard Groner. Hitler told a friend that as a small boy he most wanted to become a priest. After he had written *Mein Kampf* (*My Battle*), a text of his political and personal philosophy (including his desire to exterminate the Jews), he gave public testimony that "I am now as before a Catholic and will always remain so."[44]

In December 1941 he gave his testimony when he announced his decision to implement the Final Solution after the bombing of Pearl Harbor. He ordered that the "killings should be done as humanely as possible." This was in line with his conviction that he was observing God's injunction to cleanse the world of vermin. He carried within him the Catholic teaching that Jews were Christ-killers. The mass extermination, therefore, could be carried out without a twinge of conscience, because he was merely acting as the avenging hand of God.[45]

The Jewish people believe Hitler was a Christian because the princes of the church scrambled to secure his favor. "Hitler knows how to guide the ship," announced Monsignor Ludwig Kaas. "Even before he was Chancellor, I met him frequently and was greatly impressed by his clear thinking, by his way of facing realities while upholding his ideals, which are noble. . . . It matters little who rules so long as order is maintained."[46]

The Vatican was so appreciative of being recognized as a full partner in his efforts that it asked God to bless the Reich. On a more practical level, it ordered German bishops to swear allegiance to the Nationalist Socialist regime. The oath concluded with these significant words: "In the performance of my spiritual office and in my solicitude for the welfare and interest of the German Reich, I will endeavor to avoid all detrimental acts that might endanger it."[47]

Perhaps the Jewish people consider Hitler a Christian because the Roman church honored Hitler on his fiftieth birthday. Special votive masses were celebrated in every German church "to implore God's blessing upon the Führer and the people." The pope also sent his congratulations.[48]

During World War II, the church bells of Europe rang for Hitler's birthday and his military victories. His picture hung in every Roman Catholic school in the Third Reich. When an assassination attempt on Hitler's demonized life failed, the pope sent a letter stating that God had spared his life. The Catholic press throughout the Reich piously declared that it "was the miraculous working of Providence which had protected the Führer."[49] Cardinal Innitzer of

Vienna pledged his loyalty to the Third Reich and asked Austrians to join Hitler in his "holy cause."

When Hitler's war machine crushed the brave but ill-prepared Polish army, Nazi newspapers carried a photo of the debris with a Scripture quoted beneath: "The Lord defeated them with horse, horsemen, and chariot."[50] When Hitler gave speeches in public, he was anointed with a supernatural demonic spirit in which he quoted sacred Scripture to justify his messianic mission to purge Germany and Europe of the Jews "once and for all." His mesmerizing voice thundered over the heads of his electrified audience as he proclaimed, "I'm doing the will of God."

After more than forty years following the Allies' liberation of the Jews from Auschwitz, not one word of official condemnation or excommunication concerning Hitler has been expressed by the Vatican. Why? Because six million people were murdered by baptized Christians in good standing with the church.

During our generation, one-third of the Jews of Europe were choked to death on Zyklon-B gas. On July 20, 1933, as Hitler signed the Concordant of Collaboration with the Vatican, he said, "I am only continuing the work of the Catholic Church, to isolate the Jews and fight their influence." Hitler later described the Concordant as an "unrestricted acceptance of National Socialism by the Vatican."

The bishops of Austria and Germany blessed the swastika flags of the Third Reich and pledged their loyalty "voluntarily and without duress." The Vicar of Christ looked out his window from the Vatican and watched the Nazis drag helpless women and innocent Jewish children from their homes, and load them like cattle into trucks for transport to a death of horror in the extermination camps.

What happened to those Jewish children? Read these reports from the Nuremberg trials:

> They killed them with their parents, in groups and alone. They killed them in children's homes and hospitals, burying them alive and in graves, throwing them into flames, stabbing them with bayonets, poisoning them, conducting experiments upon them, extracting their blood for the use of the German army, throwing them into prison and Gestapo torture chambers and concentration camps where the children died from hunger, torture, and epidemic diseases.[51]

> Very frequently women would hide their children under their clothes, but of course when we found them we would send the children in to be exterminated.[52]

> Mothers in the throes of childbirth shared cars with those infected with tuberculosis or venereal disease. Babies, when born, were hurled out of these cars' windows.[53]

> At that time, when the greatest number of Jews were exterminated in the gas chambers, an order was issued that the children were to be thrown into the crematory ovens, or into the crematory ditches, without previous asphyxiation with gas. . . . The children were thrown in alive; their cries could be heard all over the camp.[54]

If Jesus and his family, all Jews, had lived in Berlin, Germany, in 1940, they would have been prodded into cattle cars at bayonet point and shipped to Auschwitz.

Arriving at Auschwitz, they would have been ushered into a gas chamber en masse to scratch and claw at the walls in terror as they frantically gasped for breath. The gas chamber was camouflaged as a shower—an ordinary room, but fitted with airtight doors and windows, into which gas piping had been laid. The compressed-gas containers and the regulating equipment were located outside and operated by the Nazi doctors on duty.

Jesus Christ, along with Mary, Joseph, James, and John, would have been led into the gas chambers on the pretext that they needed a shower after their long train ride from Berlin to Auschwitz. They would have slowly choked to death on the gas for fifteen long minutes, still standing grotesquely erect because they were packed too tightly to fall. In dying, their bodies would have been covered with sweat and urine. Their legs would have been smeared with feces. This Nazi Final Solution would have been carried out by men whose leaders told them, "This is the will of God."

After death, the teeth of Jesus and His family would have been broken out with pliers or hammers in a search for gold fillings, their hair cut off to make mattresses, their flesh skinned for Nazi lamp shades. Their remains would have been thrown into an oven and cremated, the stench belching out through massive smokestacks that covered the countryside.

That night, the skies of Auschwitz would glow red with the ashes of dead Jews, the family of our Lord. Those ashes were often used to make soap or fertilizer for the Third Reich. Think of it! Fertilizing your roses with the ashes of the Virgin Mary, soaping your body with the remains of the apostle John, sleeping on a mattress of human hair provided by the apostle Peter.

But Hitler and his cronies couldn't see the Jews as the family of Jesus Christ. According to Hitler, Jesus was the first Jew hater. "Christ was the greatest early fighter in the battle against the world enemy, the Jews," Hitler ranted.[55]

Hitler knew that when his goose-stepping killers knelt to pray in Saint Matthew's Cathedral, they must not see Saint

Matthew as Jewish. How could they possibly leave the sanctuary of worship and then savagely machine-gun Jews in an open ditch? How could they kneel at the statue of the Virgin Mary holding the Christ child in her arms and then mercilessly slaughter one and a half million Jewish babies?

The mystery is solved by Hitler's own words. In 1927, when he dictated *Mein Kampf* to his aide, he ended his work by saying, "The great masses of the people . . . will more easily fall victims to a great lie than to a small one."[56]

Russian Anti-Semitism

The Russian word *pogrom,* which pertains to the massacre of a helpless people, passed into the international lexicon after the devastation of the Jews in the Ukraine in 1903. The Russian nation has been persecuting Jews since the time of the czars. In the span of time between the two world wars, the entire Jewish population of the Russian Western War Zone—including the old, sick, and children—were forcibly evacuated into the interior of the country on twelve hours' notice.

In August 1924 *Dawn* magazine reported:

> Wholesale slaughter and burials alive, rape and torture, became not merely commonplace but the order of the day. There were pogroms that lasted a week; and in several cases the systematic and diabolic torture and outrage and carnage were continued for a month. In many populous Jewish communities there were no Jewish survivors left to bury the dead, and thousands of Jewish wounded and killed were eaten by dogs and pigs; in others the Synagogues were turned into charnel houses by the pitiless butchery of those who sought refuge in them. If we add to the figures quoted above the number of those indirect victims who in consequence of the robbery

and destruction that accompanied these massacres were swept away by famine, disease, exposure and all manner of privations—the death total will be very near half a million human beings.[57]

Twenty years later, Hermann Grabe was an eyewitness to what happened at Dulmo, a city in the Ukraine. On October 5, 1942, Grabe went to his office in Dulmo and was told by his foreman that all the Jews in the neighborhood were being exterminated. Approximately 1,500 were being shot each day in massive ditches.

Grabe and his foreman drove to the execution ditches. As they arrived, Nazi SS troops with dogs and whips were driving Jews off packed trucks and toward the trenches. Grabe described the scene this way:

> The Jews were ordered to strip. They were told to put down their clothes in tidy order, boots and shoes, top clothing and underclothing. Already there were great piles of this clothing and a heap of eight hundred to a thousand pairs of boots and shoes. The people undressed. The mothers undressed their little children, without screaming or weeping. They had reached a point of human suffering where tears no longer flow and all hope has been abandoned. They stood around in family groups, kissed each other, said farewells, and waited. They were waiting for a signal from the SS man with a whip, who was standing by the pit. They stood there waiting for a quarter of an hour, waiting for their turn to come, while on the other side of the earthen mound, now that the shots were no longer heard, the dead and the dying were being packed into the pit. . . .
>
> I heard no complaints, no appeal for mercy. I watched a family of about eight persons, a man and a woman both about fifty, with their grown-up children, about twenty to twenty-four. An old woman with snow-white

hair was holding a little baby in her arms, singing to it and tickling it. The baby was cooing with delight. The couple were looking at each other with tears in their eyes. The father was holding the hand of a boy about ten years old and speaking to him softly; the boy was fighting his tears.[58]

These Jewish people were marched into the execution ditch and shot in the back of the head in the usual Nazi fashion, under orders from a man who claimed to follow the Christ of the Cross.

The Cross of Oppression

What do you think of when you see a cross? I'm reminded of the joy of redemption. I think of the Resurrection, of my beloved Lord, of hope, of eternal life. The cross, to me, is a life-affirming symbol.

But during the time of Christ, Jesus was one of between 50,000 and 100,000 Jews crucified as anti-Roman rebels in the first century. Historian Hyam Maccoby, speaking of the persecution the Jews experienced under the ancient Romans, wrote: "The cross became as much a symbol of Roman oppression as nowadays the gas chamber is a symbol of German Nazi oppression. . . . Associating the guilt of the cross with the Jews rather than the Romans is comparable to branding the Jewish victims . . . with the guilt of using gas chambers instead of suffering from them."[59]

When Christians see a cross they think of redemption and forgiveness. When a Jew sees a cross, he sees an electric chair. For him and his people, a cross has been a symbol of death for centuries.

A Russian theologian, Nikolay Berdyayev, wrote: "Perhaps the saddest thing to admit is that those who have rejected the Cross have to carry it, while those who welcomed it are as often engaged in crucifying others."[60]

We must examine the lies from ancient times and expose them to the light of truth. It is time for Christian people to cast off the vicious legacy of the past and make sure our people no longer carry hateful tales in their memories or pass them on to the next generation.

Malicious Myths About Jewish People

It's said that if you tell a lie long enough, sooner or later people will begin to believe it. Though the number-one myth about the Jewish people is that the Jews killed Jesus, other fantastic tales have abounded throughout history. Some undoubtedly sprang into being through ignorance and fear; others were malicious rumors spread in order to drive Jews away and confiscate their property.

Economic Persecution

Greed is a driving force behind much of the persecution of the Jews. Perhaps Mark Twain said it best. In the September 1898 issue of *Harper's* magazine, Twain wrote:

> I feel convinced that the Crucifixion has not much to do with the world's attitude toward the Jew; that the reasons for it are much older than that. . . . I am convinced that in Russia, Austria and Germany nine-tenths of the hostility to the Jew comes from the average Christian's inability to compete successfully with the average Jew in business.

What motivates many of those who persecute the Jews? The love of money. Greed. Jealousy for a blessing given to them by God through Abraham: "I will bless you . . . and in you all the families of the earth shall be blessed" (Gen. 12:2–3).

In the Middle Ages, for instance, many Jews were involved in banking. In 1247 Pope Innocent III wrote that Christians should pay their debts: "Although the said Jews make honest loans of their money to these Christians, the latter, in order to drain from them all their wealth . . . refuse to repay their money to them."[61]

In his letter, the pope actually complimented Jewish honesty and admitted that Christians were trying to rob them. In fact, the practice went much farther than a simple refusal to repay. Often people would borrow money from a Jew, then when the loan fell due, they would appeal to the civil or ecclesiastical authorities on the grounds that the transaction was illegal or the rate unduly exorbitant. If the appeal failed, the debtors would then circulate rumors, organize riots, knock the creditor on the head, or resort to threats and intimidation.

How many times have you heard this or a similar expression: "He tried to jew me down on the price"? I'm not certain why Jews have been characterized as having a particular lust for money when history teaches that Gentiles hungered for Jewish money! Christian body snatchers of the thirteenth century rifled through Jewish cemeteries and exhumed corpses for the purpose of extorting money from the survivors.[62] On some occasions the bones of wealthy Jews were dug up, put on trial, and pronounced guilty of heresy in what amounted to little more than a monstrous act of extortion.

Pope Gregory X had to rebuke his flock for a similar situation. Certain Christian fathers whose children had died hid the children's bodies on Jewish properties, then proceeded to extort money from the Jews by threatening to accuse them of having murdered the children to obtain blood for the Passover ceremony.[63]

The Blood-of-Christian-Children Lie

Let me tell you about a malicious myth that was far from harmless. This story began during medieval times, and it survives to this present day. Unfortunately, it has been the cause of heartbreak, endless pain, and many terrible and tragic deaths.

This story, originally concocted by a monk named Theobald, was first put into writing by Thomas of Monmouth, an English monk of the Order of Saint Benedict. Thomas heard the story of a young boy named William, who had been found dead in the woods outside the town of Norwich. Some months later, Thomas of Monmouth accused Jews of killing the boy. He said they had enticed the boy into a house, tortured him, and crucified him.

Thomas's tale did not meet with the approval of his superiors, but it caught the imagination of the populace, who used it as an excuse for attacking the so-called enemies of Christ. While Jews were tortured until they "confessed," an actual cult arose to honor Blessed William, the first child martyr. The business of venerating the child proved profitable.

Thomas's story spread like an aggressive cancer. This lie about human sacrifice influenced the king of France, Philip Augustus, who in 1182 drove the Jews out of his country because he believed they were sacrificing Christian children.

On March 26, 1247, a little girl, two years old, was found dead in a ditch outside the French town of Valréas. A rumor quickly spread that the child had been abducted by Jews and that her blood had been used in their religious ceremonies—the Passover ritual was especially suspect.

Three Jews were arrested for the child's murder. They were tortured until they confessed, then they were put to death. Many other Jews in the district were rounded up, tortured, and burned at the stake. Pope Innocent was savvy enough to recognize the motivation behind this mass murder, and he sent envoys who condemned "the cruelty of Christians who, covetous of their possessions, thirsting for their blood, despoil, torture, and kill all Jews without legal judgment."[64]

Little Saint Hugh of Lincoln

In 1255 when a boy named Hugh of Lincoln disappeared, another version of the story began to circulate. In this adaptation of William's tale, Hugh was stolen by Jews and shut up in a room for the purpose of being crucified. The boy was subjected to diverse tortures, beaten until blood flowed, and crowned with thorns. His captors crucified him and pierced his heart with a lance. After the boy expired, they took his body from the cross and disemboweled it.

Meanwhile, in Lincoln, a search team found the boy's body in a well. There was no evidence, no mark, to indicate the boy had been murdered. Yet ninety-six Jews of Lincoln were taken to London, where eighteen of the richest and most powerful were hanged.

Young Hugh, promoted to the rank of martyr, was venerated for generations as Little Saint Hugh of Lincoln. A church was dedicated to his memory, and his tomb became a famous resort for pilgrims who came to worship and pray for miracles. Chaucer even mentioned the gruesome story in his fictional *Canterbury Tales*. In "The Prioress's Tale," Chaucer has his prioress state that because a young Christian boy constantly sang hymns to the Virgin, "from thence forth the Jews conspired this innocent out of this world to chase" (spelling modernized). The Jews of her story capture this innocent Christian boy, cut his throat, and cast him into a pit. The boy dies, but not before being rescued and pledging his loyalty to the Virgin, this despite having his "throat cut to the neck bone."[65] Chaucer ends his story with a reference to "young Hugh of Lincoln, slain also with cursed Jews."

Although Little Saint Hugh was revered for generations, the entire story was what we would now call an urban legend. There was no evidence that the boy had been killed by anyone, and yet every time a young child turned up missing, Jews were routinely hauled out and put to death for "confessions" under torture.

This outrageous slander was also cited as one reason why Ferdinand and Isabella chose to drive the Jews out of Spain in 1492. The story had grown by this time, and the storytellers spoke of a child named Richard who had been crucified by the Jews, William of Norwich, Little Saint Hugh, and another child named Robert.

The myths and calumnies continue to persist. Tomáš Masaryk, the first president of Czechoslovakia, wrote:

> In the fifties of the last [nineteenth] century every Slovak child in the vicinity of Goding was nurtured in an atmosphere of anti-Semitism; in school, church and society at large. Mother would forbid us to go near the Lechners because, as she said, Jews were using the blood of Christian children. I would therefore make a wide turn to avoid passing their house; and so did all my schoolmates. . . . The superstition of Christian blood

used for Passover cakes had become so much part and parcel of my existence that whenever I chanced to come near a Jew—I wouldn't do it on purpose—I would look at his fingers to see if blood were there. . . . Would that I may unmake all that anti-Semitism caused me to do in my childhood days.[66]

In 1936, 700 years after Pope Innocent's decree condemning the lie about ritual murder, a German newspaper, *Der Stürmer*, published illustrations showing Jews sucking the blood of innocent children.[67] Is it any wonder that Nazi propaganda in Germany issued periodic warnings for families to keep their children especially close at Passover time?

Oh, you may be thinking, *no rational person today would believe such things!* I beg to disagree! Samuel Macy, a thirty-three-year-old Harvard librarian, decided in 1996 to track hate groups on the Internet. As he surfed the Web, he discovered that so-called Christian identity groups in the United States are keeping the rumors alive. Their Web pages say that Jews are the product of a union between Eve and Satan, and they also report that Jews kill Christians and use their blood to make matzo.[68] How are they different from Chaucer's prioress, who said, "Our first foe, the serpent Satan . . . hath in Jews' hearts his wasp's nest"?[69]

Those who spread rumors about the Jews and lay the blame for Christ's death at the feet of the Jewish nation have made a grave mistake. But since the formation of the nation of Israel, the Jews have suffered at the hands of tyrants, so-called Christian emperors, crusaders, self-anointed and self-serving theologians, and everyday misinformed Christians. Constant historic expressions of anti-Semitism have spawned every imaginable theological and philosophical rebuttal to the rights of Jewish people to their land, their Holy City, and their place in God's eternal plan.

As late as 1770, Voltaire, the French Enlightenment's most prominent intellectual, wrote, "Jewish priests have always sacrificed human victims with their sacred hands." He went on to add that though the Jews were the "most abominable people in the world . . . nevertheless, they should not be burned at the stake."[70]

Modern anti-Semitism lives!

For 2,000 years Christian theology has been twisted into a lie that is the cornerstone of anti-Semitism. Singing hymns of love and claiming to act as the defenders of God, the faithful have stepped over the tortured bodies of ten million Jews whom anti-Semites have labeled "the Christ-killers!"

They are wrong, my friend. Read on.

CHAPTER 5

WHO REALLY
KILLED CHRIST?

Attempting to shed some light on the staggering accounts of the Jews' persecution, Dr. James Parker
wrote, "In our own day . . . more than six million deliberate murders are the consequences of the teachings about
Jews for which the Christian Church is ultimately responsible . . . which has its ultimate resting place in the teaching of the New Testament itself."[1]

The most deadly New Testament myth is the rumor that
the Jews killed Jesus! What can we find in the New Testament to support this supposition? Absolutely nothing!

If this were a criminal investigation and we set out to
discover who *really* killed Christ, we'd consider an eyewitness account the most reliable sort of testimony. Let's look
at the biblical text closely. What do the eyewitness accounts
of Matthew, Mark, Luke, and John actually say about
Christ's crucifixion?

The Jewish writers of the Gospels took special care to
record the fact that the Jewish people, their *own* people,
were not only not responsible, but were for the most part

unaware of the events that led up to the apprehension, trial, and condemnation of Jesus Christ.

Matthew's Testimony

In the most Jewish of all the Gospels, Matthew states that the Jews, as a people, had nothing to do with the political conspiracy against Jesus. He exposes the true conspirators in chapter 26 of his book: "Then the chief priests, the scribes, and the elders of the people assembled at the palace of the high priest, who was called Caiaphas, and plotted to take Jesus by trickery and kill Him" (v. 3–4).

Two very important points are clear:

1. There was a crucifixion plot.
2. The high priest, Caiaphas, carried out the intrigue, and he in no way represented the Jewish people. He was politically appointed by Herod Antipas, who was himself directly appointed by Rome. The Jewish people hated Herod and the high priest because they were political pawns in the hands of the pagan Romans.

Herod the Great, father of Herod Antipas, rose to power through the tyrannical intervention of Roman military rule forty years before Christ was born. Rome's Mark Anthony joined military forces with Herod the Great in an attack on the city of Jerusalem. After five months, Jerusalem fell, and Mark Anthony appointed Herod as its Roman supervisor. Herod was a paranoid dictator who murdered several members of his own family. He was a notoriously jealous and insanely insecure ruler, and it was in character for him to order the slaughter of all baby boys under two years old when he feared a report by wise men from the East that a "King of the Jews" had been born (see Matt. 2:1–12).

After rising to power, Herod the Great promptly ordered forty-five members of the Jewish Sanhedrin murdered in order to gain absolute dictatorial control and to silence the Jewish voice in government. During the reigns of Herod the Great and Herod Antipas, his son, the Sanhedrin was nothing more than a pawn of the state. Herod held absolute power by the will of Rome, not by the vote of the Jewish people.

Herod also appointed the high priest, Caiaphas, leader of the Calvary conspiracy, to carry out Rome's will. Caiaphas was an illegitimate priest, not selected by the Jewish people. During the Great Revolt of A.D. 66–70, Josephus records that religious Jews burned down the high priest's house because he was a corrupt puppet of Rome.

Into this shady political setting came a Rabbi called Jesus of Nazareth. Because the Jews were looking for a deliverer to lead a revolt and break the oppressive chains of Rome, Jesus' popularity spread like lightning. Anyone who could feed 5,000 people from one boy's lunch could feed an army to defeat Rome! Anyone who could heal and raise people from the dead could heal wounded soldiers and raise dead troops back to life. The people saw Jesus as their military answer to conquer mighty Rome. Rome saw Jesus as an insurrectionist too threatening to allow to live.

Seen in this light, Jesus was a serious political threat to Herod Antipas and to his stooge, Caiaphas. Consequently, they entered into a politically motivated plot to have Jesus killed Roman style—by crucifixion. Jewish law allowed execution by stoning only. Had the Jews killed Jesus, He would have been stoned, not crucified.

The Leaders Feared a Riot

When Caiaphas met with his political pawns to consider how best to kill Jesus of Nazareth, the Scriptures state that they decided to arrest Jesus in a secretive way so they wouldn't cause a riot among the Jewish people present in the city: "[They] plotted to take Jesus by trickery and kill Him. But they said, 'Not during the feast, lest there be an uproar among the people'" (Matt. 26:4–5).

If the Jews were behind the crucifixion plot, why would they fear a riot? A riot requires the spontaneous uprising among the general population. But the high priest knew that the majority of the Jewish people supported Jesus and would spontaneously erupt in anger if He were arrested. News of a riot would travel to Rome. Herod would be politically embarrassed, and the high priest would be instantly displaced from his lucrative and powerful position.

Matthew contributes more evidence that the leaders of this plot feared the Jewish people: "But when they sought to lay hands on Him, they feared the multitudes, because they took Him for a prophet" (21:46).

Certainly some Jews were displeased with Jesus' leadership and teaching. The School of Hillel, a group of Jewish religious rabbis, was furious because Jesus endorsed their opponent Shammai's teaching on divorce. No one had to urge Hillel's followers to scream for the crucifixion of Jesus. They numbered fewer than a few hundred, but they were more than glad to betray Him or anyone else who rejected their doctrine. Some things never change.

Even after Jesus' death, the enemies of Jesus weren't finished with their plotting. Big problems developed for the local theologians when He rose from the dead on the third day. The conspirators had a lot of explaining to do. Once again, Caiaphas's moral corruption manifested itself. He paid large bribes to the guards watching the tomb and told them to lie about what had happened.

Let the eyewitness account of Matthew speak for the record: "When they [the chief priests] had assembled with the elders and consulted together, they gave a large sum of money to the soldiers, saying, 'Tell them, "His disciples came at night and stole Him away while we slept." And if this comes to the governor's ears, we will appease him and make you secure'" (28:12–14).

Note five important points:

1. The chief priests were conspirators.
2. The chief priests were guilty of offering Roman soldiers a bribe, a criminal act punishable by death.
3. The chief priests were liars who paid other people to lie.
4. The guards at the tomb could have been put to death for sleeping at their post, but the chief priests were so totally confident of their political connections that they assured the guards they could appease the governor and keep the guards out of trouble.
5. Because the chief priests' political connections to Rome were common knowledge, the guards were not afraid to accept the bribe and become part of the plot.

The actions of a single man, Caiaphas, and of his conspiring cronies hardly constitute the actions of an entire nation.

Mark and Luke Agree

Luke and Mark join Matthew in contributing evidence that these political prostitutes did not represent the Jewish people (italics mine).

And the scribes and chief priests heard it and sought how they might destroy Him; for they feared Him, *because all the people* were astonished at His teaching (Mark 11:18).

And they sought to lay hands on Him, but *feared the multitude,* for they knew He had spoken the parable against them. So they left Him and went away (Mark 12:12).

And the chief priests and the scribes sought how they might take Him by trickery and put Him to death. But they said, "Not during the feast, lest there be an *uproar of the people*" (Mark 14:1–2).

And He [Jesus] was teaching daily in the temple. But the chief priests, the scribes, and the leaders of the people sought to destroy Him, and were unable to do anything; for *all the people were very attentive to hear Him* (Luke 19:47–48).

And the chief priests and the scribes that very hour sought to lay hands on Him, but *they feared the people*—for they knew He had spoken this parable against them (Luke 20:19).

And the chief priests and the scribes sought how they might kill Him, for they *feared the people* (Luke 22:2).

Jesus Himself identified His killers before His death (italics mine): "Then He took the twelve aside and said to them, 'Behold, we are going up to Jerusalem, and all things that are written by the prophets concerning the Son of Man will be accomplished. For He will be delivered *to the Gentiles* and will be mocked and insulted and spit upon. And they will scourge Him and kill Him. And the third day He will rise again'" (Luke 18:31–33).

The biblical text is perfectly clear. Jesus was crucified by Rome as a political insurrectionist. He was a threat to Herod's authority. He was a threat to the high priest. The men of Herod's inner circle produced the Calvary conspiracy. His death had nothing to do with the Jewish people as a race, nation, or civilization.

Consider the historical facts: At the time Jesus began His ministry, three out of four Jews did not live in Israel. Nine out of ten Jews during that time lived outside Jerusalem. At most, only a few hundred irate Pharisees could have possibly participated in or supported the high priest's Calvary plot.

What About the Mob at Pilate's Mansion?

Ah, yes, how many times have we heard "proof-text" Christians rattle on about the mob who screamed, "Let Him be crucified!" and "His blood be on us and on our children" (Matt. 27:23, 25). Surely *this* Scripture proves that all Jewish people are forever guilty of the blood of Jesus Christ.

The scriptural and historical fact is that the political puppet, Caiaphas, gathered and controlled that crowd. Remember, this was an orchestrated plot, not a spontaneous expression of the people. The chief priests were frightened of an honest crowd. Matthew, the eyewitness, tells us that "the chief priests and elders persuaded the multitudes that they should ask for Barabbas and destroy Jesus" (27:20).

How did they persuade the crowd? It didn't take much. These were the Pharisees who were as mad as a nest of hornets poked with a stick. Jesus had called them "whitewashed tombs" (Matt. 23:27) and told them that casual divorce was against God's plan. They were angry, and they took their opportunity to be rid of the One causing them trouble.

You may have noticed that I didn't include any passages from John when I mentioned the eyewitness accounts of the crucifixion. That's because John's Gospel requires a different examination.

The Jews of John's Gospel

For centuries preachers in Christian pulpits read the thirty-two references to Jews in John's Gospel and concluded that all Jews are bloodthirsty torturers, pitiless killers, and money-hungry temple desecrators. Christian pulpiteers pounded their pulpits and shouted a message of hatred. They quoted verses like John 5:16 ("For this reason the Jews persecuted Jesus, and sought to kill Him, because He had done these things on the Sabbath") and John 7:1 ("After these things Jesus walked in Galilee; for He did not want to walk in Judea, because the Jews sought to kill Him").

Were *All* the Jews Guilty?

For 1,500 years, the guilt of a handful of Jews who hated Jesus has been spread with a broad brush to include all Jewish people. For centuries, Christian leaders have used the above verses, and others like them, to justify anti-Semitism.

Saint John Chrysostom, he of the golden mouth, wrote, "The Jews . . . erred not ignorantly but with full knowledge."[2] Several hundred years later, just prior to the Second Crusade, Saint Bernard of Clairvaux agreed with Chrysostom's theology. Bernard wrote: "The Jews were all guilty; they acted with deliberate malice; that their guilt was shared by the whole Jewish people, for all time, and that they, and their children's children to the last generation, were condemned to live in slavery as the servants of Christian princes."[3]

Despite the passage of 700 years, Bernard echoed Chrysostom's malice. Eight hundred years after Bernard wrote his diatribe, we see that many historical figures, including Adolf Hitler, echoed Bernard's thoughts.

The Scripture says that the Jews hated Jesusm so who were these "Jews" in John's Gospel?

Let's compare the styles of Matthew and John in the reporting of a similar incident. In Matthew 12 we read the story of the man with a withered hand. Matthew says that when Jesus healed the man on the Sabbath, "The *Pharisees* went out and plotted against Him, how they might destroy Him" (v. 14, italics mine).

John, however, in reporting a similar incident, does not use the phrase *the Pharisees*, but uses the phrase *the Jews*: "The Jews therefore said to him who was cured, 'It is the Sabbath; it is not lawful for you to carry your bed.' . . . The man departed and told the Jews that it was Jesus who had made him well. For this reason the Jews persecuted Jesus, and sought to kill Him" (5:10, 15–16).

In a careful study of Scripture, you will see that "the Jews" of John 5 are "the Pharisees" of Matthew 12—the same fellows who were constantly trying to trap Jesus in a doctrinal error.

In his account of the healing of the man blind from birth (John 9:1–15), John describes the interrogation forced upon the man by the Pharisees. When the Pharisees were not satisfied with the man's response, they went to his parents. The parents admitted their son had indeed been healed, but indicated they did not know how he had been healed. John says they avoided answering because "they feared the Jews, for the Jews had agreed already that if anyone confessed that He was Christ, he would be put out of the synagogue" (9:22).

An observant study of the Bible makes it perfectly clear that "the Pharisees" of John 9:15 are "the Jews" who had intimidated the blind man's parents. But anti-Semitic leaders gladly read these passages of Scripture and assume that by writing "the Jews," John intended to accuse an entire race of people.

Who Are the Pharisees?

Scholars estimate that there were about one million Jews in Israel at the time of Christ. Of that one million, the Pharisees numbered a little more than 6,000.[4] The Pharisees, therefore, represented *less than 1 percent* of the Jewish population of Israel.

Furthermore, the Pharisees were divided into three schools of thought. One school was led by the famous Hillel, who wandered from Babylonia to Jerusalem and joined a house of study. In time, he was recognized as one of the foremost teachers of the Pharisees. Hillel served as a patriarch in Israel from 10 B.C. until A.D. 10. He fostered a systematic, liberal, relatively lenient interpretation of Scripture, and his students ruled Jewish life for more than 400 years.

A second school of thought among the Pharisees arose under the leadership of Shammai. Shammai and Hillel could agree on virtually nothing. They constantly debated right and wrong on practically every issue.

A third school of thought was formed by the Essenes, an ascetic Jewish sect whose members lived in the Judean desert. John the Baptist could have easily belonged to this community, as could have Jesus Christ. It is very possible that in the silent years of His life, between the ages of eighteen and thirty, Jesus studied Torah at Qumran where the Dead Sea Scrolls were discovered in 1947. Qumran is only a short distance from the Jordan River, where Jesus was baptized by John. It is entirely conceivable that Jesus studied from the Dead Sea Scrolls now on display in Israel at the Shrine of the Book.

Regardless of membership in a sect, the Pharisees were set apart from the common people. The word *Pharisee* comes from the word *Perushim,* which means to be separated. These religious separatists held themselves aloof from all other Jews and from other Pharisees who did not agree with their doctrinal teaching. They were extremely careful in matters of ritual purity and refused to touch a menstruating woman, a woman who had just given birth, a corpse, a dead reptile, a leper, or anything else that smacked of being unclean.

The Pharisees believed that they alone were the rightful teachers and interpreters of the oral law. They believed in the resurrection of the dead, in angels, and in God's guidance of human events.

All three groups of Pharisees were powerful and influential. Chaim Potok wrote:

> It is an error to see these Pharisees as gentle old men with flowing white beards; see them rather as passionate followers of scribal teachings adept with sword and spear as well as with text of the law, quite willing to kill for the sake of their God. We are talking of a time when men easily took up the sword for what they held dear. The Pharisees killed for God rather than for plunder. It is to be doubted if those who fell by Pharisee swords were thereby consoled.[5]

During the time of Jesus, doctrinal disputes still raged between the followers of Hillel and Shammai concerning the law of divorce. Shammai taught that a man could not divorce his wife for just any trivial cause, but could get a divorce for fornication. (Biblically, fornication included adultery, homosexuality, bestiality, and lewdness.) For Jews, the scriptural right to divorce also included the right to remarry. This position was accepted without question throughout Israel.

Hillel was an extremist, teaching that a man could divorce his wife "for every cause." According to Hillel, a husband could divorce his wife for talking too loud, for talking too much, for failing to prepare kosher meals, for seasoning food carelessly, for going into the street with loose or uncombed hair. A husband could divorce his wife if he found a more beautiful wife, or for any other reason.

The followers of Hillel were constantly trying to lure Jesus into this raging doctrinal dispute, and the story of how they approached Him is recorded in Matthew 19:3: "The Pharisees also came to Him, testing Him, and saying to Him, 'Is it lawful for a man to divorce his wife for just any reason?'"

Jesus knew His life was on the line. If He disagreed with those sword-carrying legalists, they would try to kill Him.

Jesus searched their hearts, looked them in the eye, and gave this answer: "Moses, because of the hardness of your hearts, permitted you to divorce your wives, but from the beginning it was not so. And I say to you, whoever divorces his wife, except for sexual immorality, and marries another, commits adultery; and whoever marries her who is divorced commits adultery" (Matt. 19:8–9).

With the utterance of those words, the fight was on! From that moment Jesus was seen as a living devil to the Pharisees who followed Hillel. They plotted to have Him killed. These were "the Jews" that Jesus said were of their "father the devil." These are "the Jews" that interrogated the parents of the blind man until they shook with fear. These are "the Jews" from whom Jesus' disciples were hiding behind closed doors. These are "the Jews" that Christians have used for 2,000 years to condone religious hatred, rape, murder, and execution.

But we can't assume that all the Pharisees opposed Jesus. Many Pharisees were friends of Jesus. They loved Him, He ate with them, and they tried to save His life.

Jesus' Pharisee Friends

In John's Gospel we read of Nicodemus, who went to Jesus "by night." Entirely too much criticism has been heaped upon Nicodemus for going to Jesus after dark as if he were sneaking around. Nothing could be farther from the truth. Nicodemus was a ruler of the Pharisees and was in the courts all day. The only logical time to see Jesus was after sundown.

Nicodemus did not hesitate to confess, "Rabbi, we know that You are a teacher come from God; for no one can do these signs that You do unless God is with him" (3:2).

Nicodemus admired and stood in awe of Jesus. He thought enough of Jesus to seek His opinions; he thought enough of Jesus to later bring 100 pounds of valuable myrrh and aloes to help with the burial of Jesus' body (19:39).

Nicodemus was not the only Pharisee to befriend Jesus. Though we do not have the names of others, we know that Jesus ate with Pharisees (Luke 7:37), an act that brought Him sharp criticism. In biblical times, you did not break bread with a man unless a bond of mutual esteem and respect existed between the two of you. In fact, betraying a man or speaking ill of him after eating with him was the ultimate act of disloyalty. It was unthinkable to eat with someone and then entrap him. King David once lamented: "Even my own familiar friend in whom I trusted, / Who ate my bread, / Has lifted up his heel against me" (Psalm 41:9).

Obviously, many Pharisees dined with Jesus and would not have done so without intending to support Him to the death.

What About Judas?

Because Judas betrayed Jesus as they were eating the Last Supper together, the name *Judas* has become the universal synonym for "traitor." So wasn't at least this specific Jew to blame for Jesus' death?

No. Judas was not an ethnic Jew. The church fathers who have called him "Jew-das" were in error.

Jesus chose twelve disciples. Only ten were necessary for a Jewish minyan, the minimum number required before religious services could be conducted. Ten of Christ's disciples were ethnic and religious Jews. Judas Iscariot and Simon the Canaanite were not ethnic Jews, but religious proselytes.

"Iscariot" was not Judas's last name. *Ish-Kirot* means he was a foreigner, an alien to the ethnic family of Israel. *Ish* means "man" and *Kirot* means he was a citizen of Kir or Kirot. Kirot was a Jewish city in southern Judea. In southern Moab across the Dead Sea, another Kir or Kirot existed. If Judas had been from the Kirot in Judea, his name would have been Judas Mi-Kirot, as Mary from Migdol was called Mary Magdalene. Since Judas was a foreigner, his name was Ish-Kirot.

In the Calvary plot, Judas the foreigner and Herod the Idumaean Jew (another foreigner) had common interest in the death of Christ. Some scholars believe that Judas was Herod's spy in the ministry of Jesus Christ from day one.

Why did Judas ask for thirty pieces of silver out of the nonnegotiable shekels of the temple treasury? As a devout Jew, he could not have spent the money. As devout Jews, the temple officials could not give Judas the money. Yet they did. The collusion suggests a long-standing connection between Judas, Herod, and Herod's politically appointed high priest, Caiaphas.

Herod and the Pharisees

Further scriptural evidence that many Pharisees supported Jesus is found in Luke 13:31: "On that very day some Pharisees came, saying to Him, 'Get out and depart from here, for Herod wants to kill You.'"

These Pharisees came to warn Jesus that Herod was angry and would kill Him just as he executed John the Baptist. Everyone in Israel knew Herod was a cold-blooded murderer—he had killed nine of his ten wives. If the Pharisees had wanted Jesus dead, warning Him was the last thing they would have done. Instead, they came to alert Jesus in an effort to save His life.

John's Gospel further demonstrates how the Pharisees were divided over Christ's ministry. The situation becomes clear in the story of Jesus healing the blind man by mixing clay with saliva.

Why did Jesus spit on the ground? Because Jews of the first century believed there was healing power in the spittle of the firstborn male of every family. By His action, Jesus was testifying to all that He was the firstborn of the Father, the only begotten Son of God.

"Therefore some of the Pharisees said, 'This Man is not from God, because He does not keep the Sabbath.' Others said, 'How can a man who is a sinner do such signs?' And there was a division among them" (9:16).

Nothing in Scripture indicates a unified Jewish front to oppose Jesus. On the contrary, many Pharisees confessed that He was a Man sent from God. They followed Him to the crest of Calvary.

So Why Are the Jews Blamed for the Crucifixion?

Anti-Semitism is a demonic spirit from the bowels of hell. I believe it is designed to torment the Jewish people for bringing the torch of truth, the Word of God, and the Light of the World into a void of spiritual darkness. Hate is a cancer on the intellect and pollutes the mind. Violence flames from the embers of malice like fire flashes from intense heat. No ethnic group knows this better than the Seed of Abraham.

The Jews are blamed for so many things, often without logical reasons, for the same reason that a successful businessman or a handsome youth is hated and envied by his peers. The nation of Israel is blessed; it has been chosen by God.

"For you are a holy people to the LORD your God," Moses wrote concerning Israel, "and the LORD has chosen you to be a people for Himself, a special treasure above all the peoples who are on the face of the earth" (Deut. 14:2).

Why did God choose the nation of Israel for His own? The answer to this question is bound up in God's purpose for Israel. When God promised Abraham that he would become the father of a great nation, He also promised that He would bless all peoples through that nation.

Israel was to be a channel of blessing as well as a recipient. Even their miraculous deliverance from Egypt was partially designed to show other nations that Israel's God was the only true God. Isaiah further prophesied that the Messiah would bring salvation to the Gentiles (Isa. 49:6). The life, ministry, and death of Jesus Christ all came through Israel as God's chosen channel of blessing.

The Jews have been tested, and they know how to exhibit courage. The test of *courage* arises when we are in the minority. The test of *tolerance* arises when we are in the majority. Jesus taught, "You shall love your neighbor as yourself" (Matt. 22:39). It is not possible for a person to say "I am a Christian" and not love the Jewish people.

So—Who Is to Blame?

Should we reserve our anger and hatred, then, for *certain* Pharisees and one politically controlled high priest? No, for in the last breath of His earthly life, Jesus forgave even those who plotted against Him, saying, "Father, forgive them, for they do not know what they do" (Luke 23:34). If God has forgiven that handful of Jews who participated in the Calvary conspiracy to crucify Christ, why can't Christians?

Who is responsible for the death of Jesus Christ? The simple answer, my friend, is that we are. Though we may not have been present during those clandestine meetings when the Calvary conspiracy was launched, and though we did not bargain for the Savior's life or surrender Him for a bag of silver, it was your need, and my need, that led the Savior to Calvary.

Jesus' life wasn't taken from Him—He willingly surrendered it. Jesus told His followers, "As the Father knows Me, even so I know the Father; and I lay down My life for the sheep. . . . Therefore My Father loves Me, because I lay down My life that I may take it again. *No one takes it from Me, but I lay it down of Myself.* I have power to lay it down, and I have power to take it again" (John 10:15, 17–18, italics mine).

Why should we care for the people of Jerusalem? Because Jesus said, "Assuredly, I say to you, inasmuch as you did it to one of the least of these My brethren, you did it to Me" (Matt. 25:40). Jesus' reference to "My brethren" was a reference to the Jewish people, not some Christian denomination. In Scripture, Jesus referred to Gentiles as "dogs" (Matt. 15:26–27), not as "My brethren."

Paul paints a bleak portrait of the spiritual position of Gentiles prior to the Cross when he wrote, "At that time you were without Christ, being aliens from the commonwealth of Israel and strangers from the covenants of promise, having no hope and without God in the world" (Eph. 2:12). But through salvation in Christ, we are given the opportunity to be adopted into the family of God. "But as many as received Him," wrote the apostle John, "to them He gave the right to become children of God, to those who believe in His name: who were born, not of blood, nor of the will of the flesh, nor of the will of man, but of God" (John 1:12–13).

In the same way a tangerine branch is grafted onto an orange tree to bear fruit, the Gentiles of the world were grafted into the blessings of Abraham through the blood atonement of a Rabbi, Jesus of Nazareth.

As a Gentile, I was guaranteed death, but Jesus, a Rabbi, went to the cross and gave me eternal life.

As a Gentile, I was guaranteed sickness, but by the stripes on the back of a Rabbi, I am healed.

As a Gentile, I was guaranteed depression, despair, and death, but a Rabbi gave His life that I might have joy unspeakable and peace that surpasses understanding. I have substituted garments of praise for the spirit of heaviness. I have acquired eternal life.

As a Gentile, I was an alien, an outcast far outside the commonwealth of Israel. Jesus grafted me into the royal family of God, and now all the blessings of Abraham are mine.

As a Gentile, I was guaranteed rejection, but through Jesus, God the Father adopted me and made me a joint heir with Christ.

All He had, I got; all I had, He took.

I took His wealth; He took my poverty.

I took His forgiveness; He took my sin and shame.

I took His love and acceptance; He took my rejection.

I took His healing; He took my sickness.

I took His power; He took my fear and weakness.

Jesus Christ paid a debt He did not owe, and I owed a debt I could not pay. At Calvary a Rabbi extended His nail-pierced hand to every Gentile who was cut off, without God, and without hope. He grafted us into the blessings of Abraham. Calvary was not caused by the Jews. It was pre-destined by God "from the foundation of the world" for us (Rev. 13:8).

Hallelujah for the Cross.

CHAPTER 6

HAS GOD REJECTED THE JEWS?

As I examined the onslaught of hate historically vented toward Israel and the Jews, I wondered what prompted these Christian attacks. Why would theologians in the first millennium, during medieval times, and in this century unleash such persistent and violent assaults? Aside from the malicious myths we've already discussed, some idea, proposition, or declaration had to have begun this avalanche of hate. As I searched, it didn't take long to find and identify the poisoned spring—replacement theology.

This heresy of hatred is being taught in Sunday schools to impressionable young minds. A generation of American children is growing up believing that heartless Jews captured and crucified the Only begotten Son of God. Anti-Semitism is again being proclaimed by bellicose clerics as a Christian virtue. These preachers claim they are "defending the faith" and "fighting the devil" when they attack the Jews.

Adolf Hitler felt the same way. He said, "I am acting in accordance with the will of the Almighty Creator: by defending myself against the Jew, I am fighting for the work of the Lord."[1]

Most evangelicals believe the Jews rejected Jesus as Messiah and therefore qualify for God's eternal judgment. Replacement theologians write, "The covenant with Israel was broken because she would not accept Jesus Christ whom God sent."[2]

In the first century, theological anti-Semitism began teaching that "the church is the new Israel." Gentile converts resented the priority of the Jewish people in God's economy. A spirit of arrogance and pride causes this theology of hate to still flourish today. The concept appeals to the ego.

Hitler sold this idea to the German people, screaming to his enraptured audience, "We are the true people of God." On the other side of the globe, the Japanese called themselves the "sons of heaven." Of course, every American knows they are both wrong because God loves *us* best. Surely He's sitting on His throne waving the Stars and Stripes.

I'm kidding. You can see how foolish the God-loves-us-best concept is. But listen to the message coming from so many pulpits of America's 192 flavors of Christianity. The theme is very clear: "God loves my denomination best." Although narcissistic theology is a cancer of the soul, replacement theology is music to the ego.

The biblical truth is that our Father in heaven loves us all. He is not the enemy of my enemies. God is not even the enemy of His foes, for the Bible teaches to "love your enemies." It's a shocking thought, but God even loves the people who are in a different denomination.

As soon as we adopt the ego-gratifying idea that we are the only people of God, we are delighted to turn on the Jews because the Bible plainly identifies them as the "chosen people." We can't both be "the only people of God."

Replacement theology is not a new revelation; it's an old heresy. In his *Epistles,* Ignatius of Antioch, a Christian martyr who died in the first century, presented the church as "the new Israel." He also portrayed the prophets and heroes of Israel as "Christians before their time" and not part of the Jewish religion. Interestingly enough, this early church scholar had no trouble portraying Balaam, Absalom, and Judas as real Jews.

Replacement theologians must use the allegorical method of interpreting Scripture to support this position. This method, which was first taught in Alexandria and is based on the Platonic doctrine of ideas, spiritualizes the biblical text and purports to plumb hidden spiritual significance, yet it completely avoids the historical and literal meaning. Using the allegorical method of biblical interpretation, you can create a theology that says anything you want it to say. It's not truth; it's completely without biblical foundation. It's God's Word twisted to tell a lie.

Any group teaching that the church is the new Israel must use the allegorical method to justify their position. It is not possible to examine the literal statements of the Bible and conclude that God is finished with Israel and that the church has taken its place. Scripture plainly indicates that the church and national Israel exist side by side and that neither replaces the other—not yesterday, not today, not tomorrow.

Paul emphatically answers once and for all the question when he writes, "Has God cast away His people? Certainly not! . . . God has not cast away His people whom

He foreknew" (Rom. 11:1–2). This thought is so important that Paul addresses it a second time in the same chapter, saying, "Have they [Israel] stumbled that they should
fall? Certainly not! But through their fall, to provoke them
to jealousy, salvation has come to the Gentiles" (v. 11).

Did the Jews Reject Jesus as Messiah?

Did the Jews of Jesus' day reject Him as Messiah? Let's
examine the biblical record.

Some Jewish sages taught that there are two aspects of
the same Messiah in Scripture—a suffering Messiah (the
Lamb of God) and a reigning Messiah (the Lion of Judah).
In the biblical text, it is clear that this is the same Messiah
making two different appearances.

Oppressed by Rome, the Jews of Jesus' day were only
looking for the reigning Messiah. The crucified Nazarene
didn't fit their idea of a triumphant Messiah. This blindness to the true identity of the Messiah was sent from God
to the Jewish people (Deut. 29:4; Isa. 6:9; Jer. 5:21; Ezek.
12:2; Matt. 13:14–15; and John 12:40) and has not been
lifted to this date.

Why? Because if the Jewish people had accepted the
suffering Messiah, every Gentile would have been forever
lost. Paul confirms this by saying, "Through their fall . . .
salvation has come to the Gentiles" (Rom. 11:11).

The failure to see the suffering Jesus as the true Messiah was God's sovereign plan from the dawning of eternity so the Gentiles might have the opportunity of redemption.
Paul says that "God has committed them all to disobedience, that He might have mercy on all" (Rom. 11:32).

God's Will for Jesus

Anyone who reads the Bible knows that no man or nation can change God's sovereign will. That is also true about the life of Jesus Christ. What was God's sovereign will for His life?

The Holy Spirit spoke through Simeon in the Gospel of Luke:

> So he [Simeon] came by the Spirit into the temple. And when the parents brought in the Child Jesus, to do for Him according to the custom of the law, he took Him up in his arms and blessed God and said:
> "Lord, now You are letting Your servant depart in peace,
> According to Your word;
> For my eyes have seen Your salvation
> Which You have prepared before the face of all peoples,
> A light to bring *revelation to the Gentiles*,
> And the glory of Your people Israel" (2:27–32, italics mine).

God the Holy Spirit announced through a Jewish prophet, Simeon, that the sovereign purpose for Jesus' life was to be a "light to the Gentiles." (See also Isa. 42:6.)

This was a shocking revelation because the Jews considered the Gentiles unclean. Gentiles were "aliens from the commonwealth of Israel and strangers from the covenants of promise, having no hope and without God in the world" (Eph. 2:12).

The disciples' prejudice against the "unclean" polytheistic Gentiles was so strong that it took a divine rebuke from the angel of the Lord to get Peter to share the gospel with Gentiles in the home of Cornelius (Acts 10:19–20). That's why Jesus commanded His disciples to "preach the gospel to every creature" (Mark 16:15). Gentiles were considered creatures.

John the Baptist Speaks

As Jesus came to the Jordan River to be baptized, John the Baptist told his listeners, "Behold! The Lamb of God who takes away the sin of the world!" (John 1:29). Every listening Jew understood the symbolism behind John's words. There was only one thing to do with a young, male lamb—kill it. John was stating that the primary purpose for Jesus' life was the Cross, not a crown. He spoke of Jesus' death, not of His diadem.

John the Revelator joins the parade of witnesses by describing Jesus as "the Lamb slain from the foundation of the world" (Rev. 13:8). From the dawning of time, God intended for Jesus to die. Had Jesus permitted Himself to become the Jews' reigning Messiah, He would have missed God's sovereign will for His life.

The Crisis Theory

Replacement theologians have created a crisis theory that's the catch-22 of the New Testament. The theory goes like this: God had Plan A and Plan B for the life of Jesus Christ. Plan A was for Jesus to be Messiah of Israel. Plan B was the Cross of Calvary. Since the Jews rejected Jesus as Messiah, God had no choice but to go to Plan B, the crucifixion.

That idea is utter rubbish. First, a sovereign and almighty God is not subject to the whims and choices of man. Second, the biblical text plainly indicates that God's plan, *from the beginning*, was for Jesus to die.

Jesus knew God's plan for His life. When Jesus spoke to Nicodemus, He said, "And as Moses lifted up the serpent in the wilderness, even so must the Son of Man be lifted up, that whoever believes in Him should not perish but have eternal life" (John 3:14–15). This was a clear reference to His coming death on the cross.

When Mary of Bethany anointed Jesus' feet, He said, "She has come beforehand to anoint My body for burial" (Mark 14:8). Jesus told His disciples, "Thus it is written, and thus it was necessary for the Christ to suffer and to rise from the dead the third day" (Luke 24:46). The biblical text makes it clear that God's will was for Jesus to die on the cross, and Jesus carried out that assignment with joy.

Since Jesus was so clear about the purpose of His life, why didn't the Jews accept Him as Messiah? Consider this:

- If it was God's will for Jesus to die from the beginning,
- and if it was Jesus' intention to be obedient unto death,
- if there is not one verse of Scripture in the New Testament that says Jesus came to be the *reigning* Messiah, and
- if Jesus refused by His words and actions to claim His throne as Messiah, then *the Jews cannot be blamed for rejecting what was never offered.*

Give Us a Sign!

The Jews demanded to know if Jesus was the Messiah, and yet He steadfastly refused to answer their demands. Consider biblical history. The Jews were accustomed to their leaders demonstrating their call from God with supernatural signs. When God called Moses to go into Egypt and lead millions of Hebrew slaves out of bondage, God gave

Moses four signs with which to convince the Israelites that he was the one chosen to lead them.

The first sign God gave Moses was the miracle of the shepherd's rod that became a snake. This sign convinced Moses as well as the people. Any nagging doubts Moses might have held vanished when he saw that serpent wriggling on the ground.

The next two signs were the affliction and healing of leprosy. God told Moses to put his hand in his bosom. He did, and it instantly became white with leprosy. God ordered Moses to put his hand in his bosom a second time, and when he pulled it out, his hand was restored "like his other flesh" (Ex. 4:7).

God continues His instructions to Moses by saying, "Then it will be, if they do not believe you, nor heed the message of the first sign, that they may believe the message of the latter sign. And it shall be, if they do not believe even these two signs, or listen to your voice, that you shall take water from the river and pour it on the dry land. The water which you take from the river will become blood on the dry land" (Ex. 4:8–9).

With these four signs, Moses convinced the children of Israel that he was God's anointed leader.

If God intended Jesus to be the Messiah of Israel, why didn't He authorize Jesus to use supernatural signs to prove He was God's Anointed One? Knowing of Moses' signs to Israel, the Jews asked for a supernatural sign to indicate that Jesus was the Anointed One.

"An evil and adulterous generation seeks after a sign," Jesus said, rebuking them, "and no sign will be given to it except the sign of the prophet Jonah. For as Jonah was three days and three nights in the belly of the great fish, so will the Son of Man be three days and three nights in the heart of the earth" (Matt. 12:39–40).

Jesus refused to give a sign. He compared Himself only to the prophet Jonah, who carried God's message of repentance to the Gentiles at Nineveh. Jesus was saying, "I have come to carry a message from God to the Gentiles, and just as Jonah was in the whale's belly for three days and three nights, I will be in My grave for three days and three nights."

Jesus also invoked Jonah's name when He gave Peter a special commission to the Gentiles. He told Peter, "Blessed are you, Simon Bar-Jonah" (Matt. 16:17). *Bar-Jonah* means "son of Jonah." Jesus wasn't referring to Simon's father, whose name was Jonah, but to the prophet Jonah who reluctantly carried God's message to the Gentiles at Nineveh. Peter was the Jewish messenger who would, as a "Jonah," carry the gospel message to the Gentiles in the house of Cornelius.

The Jews were not the only people to ask for a sign. When Jesus went on trial for His life, Herod Antipas was "exceedingly glad; for he had desired for a long time to see Him, because he had heard many things about Him, and he hoped to see some miracle done by Him" (Luke 23:8). If Jesus had wanted to install Himself as the reigning Messiah of Israel, it would have been a simple matter for Him to work signs and wonders before this king. But Jesus refused to produce a sign for Herod because it was not the Father's will. Jesus' repeated response to the Jewish people who urged Him to be their Messiah was "My kingdom is not of this world" (John 18:36).

"Tell No Man"

If Jesus wanted to be the reigning Messiah, why did He repeatedly tell His disciples and followers to "tell no man" about His supernatural accomplishments? Think about it.

If He were trying to gain national attention to rally public support for the overthrow of Rome, He would not go around the country admonishing people to keep quiet.

He would have conducted Himself like any other politician, taking advantage of any and all opportunities for public exposure. The point of the political game is to *create public awareness of your cause,* to let people know who you are and what you propose to do.

But what did Jesus do?

On sixty-four occasions in the four Gospels, Jesus threw a wet blanket over His popularity, instructing those who were excited about His being Messiah to "tell no man." The people *wanted* Him to be their triumphant Messiah, but He absolutely refused.

When Jesus healed the leper, He instructed the man, "See that you tell no one; but go your way" (Matt. 8:4). When He raised Jairus's daughter from the dead, He charged the parents of the dead girl to tell no one what had happened (Luke 8:56). When He opened deaf ears, He commanded them that they should tell no one (Mark 7:36). When He healed the blind man at Bethsaida by spitting on his eye, He ordered him, saying, "Neither go into the town, nor tell anyone in the town" (Mark 8:26). When Jesus healed two blind men at once, He sternly warned them, "See that no one knows it" (Matt. 9:30).

When impetuous Peter could stand the mystery no longer, he blurted out, "You are the Christ" (Mark 8:29). You are the Anointed One, You are the Messiah that will lead the Jews in their revolt against Rome!

Jesus commanded His disciples, "that they should tell no one about Him" (Mark 8:30).

At the Transfiguration, Peter, James, and John heard Moses and Elijah talking to Jesus. They trembled as the voice of God spoke from a great cloud, saying, "This is My beloved Son. Hear Him!" And as they came down the mountain, Jesus commanded "that they should tell no one the things they had seen, till the Son of Man had risen from the dead" (Mark 9:7, 9).

Why did Jesus constantly command those who were excited about His supernatural power to "tell no man" prematurely? Because He did not come to be the reigning Messiah!

There were many Jews who would have followed Jesus when He fed 5,000 with two biscuits and five sardines! There were others who would have gladly pledged their lives when He raised Lazarus from the dead. But He performed these miracles to minister to the needs of the people, not to prove He was the Messiah.

The multiplied thousands who followed Jesus did not surrender the idea that He would be their reigning Messiah until they saw Him hanging from a Roman cross. Even after His resurrection and His repeated denials that He would not be the Messiah they expected, His disciples were still clinging to the last thread of hope that He would now smash Rome. "Lord," they asked Him, "will You at this time restore the kingdom to Israel?" (Acts 1:6).

The Jews who followed Jesus wanted Him to be their reigning Messiah, but He flatly refused.

The Jewish Mother

The mother of disciples James and John had her own ideas about Jesus' role as Messiah. Right up until the shadow of His cross fell across the bloody sands of Calvary, she tried to get Jesus to agree to place her two sons at His right and left hand when He established His kingdom (Matt. 20:20–23). She was not thinking about the suffering Messiah or a Roman cross; she wanted positions of influence and power for her sons in an earthly political kingdom. When Jesus defeated Rome as the reigning Jewish Messiah, she wanted her sons in positions of prominence.

What was Jesus' response? He looked at her and said, "You do not know what you ask" (Matt. 20:22). "The Son of Man did not come to be served, but to serve, and to give His life a ransom for many" (Matt. 20:28).

The Disciples on the Emmaus Road

The two disciples on the road to Emmaus (a settlement located seven miles outside Jerusalem) wanted Jesus to be the reigning Messiah. As they walked, Jesus Himself joined them on the road, but they did not recognize Him.

Jesus asked, "What kind of conversation is this that you have with one another as you walk and are sad?" (Luke 24:17).

The one named Cleopas answered, "Are You the only stranger in Jerusalem, and have You not known the things which happened there in these days?" (Luke 24:18).

Jesus answered, "What things?" (Luke 24:19).

"Concerning Jesus of Nazareth," they answered, "who was a Prophet mighty in deed and word before God and all the people. . . . The chief priests and our rulers delivered Him to be condemned to death, and crucified Him. *But we were hoping that it was He who was going to redeem Israel*" (Luke 24:19–21, italics mine).

Those two disciples on the road to Emmaus had not rejected Jesus as Messiah—their hopes were dashed! It was not until Jesus entered their house for fellowship that they recognized Him. When He sat at their table, lifting His hands to bless and break the bread, they saw His nail-scarred hands and recognized Jesus. Instantly, He disappeared! He refused to be their reigning Messiah, choosing instead to be the Savior of the world.

Jesus Declines the Cup

As Jesus celebrated His last Passover with His disciples, He rejected, for the final time, the Messiahship of Israel.

Let me explain: It has been my privilege to join the Orthodox Synagogue in San Antonio in the celebration of Passover with Rabbi Arnold Scheinberg. Four cups of wine are served at the Passover with a meal that symbolizes the tears and suffering of the Hebrew slaves in Egypt.

- The first cup is the cup of Remembrance.
- The second cup is the cup of Redemption.
- The third cup is the cup of Salvation.
- The fourth cup is the cup of Messiah.

When Jesus and His disciples came to the final cup during their celebration of the Passover, Jesus *refused to drink* from the Messiah's cup. Instead He took it, gave thanks, and told His disciples, "Take this and divide it among yourselves; for I say to you, I will not drink of the fruit of the vine until the kingdom of God comes" (Luke 22:17–18).

In refusing to drink from the cup, Jesus rejected to the last detail the role of Messiah in word or deed. The Jews did not reject Jesus as Messiah; Jesus rejected the Jewish desire for Him to be their reigning Messiah. He was the Lamb of God. He had come to die, but even at that point the disciples were not ready to see the truth.

Two Israels

The scriptural portraits of two Messiahs—one suffering, one reigning—depict Jesus Christ as He came and as He will come. In a similar manner, Scripture describes and defines two Israels: One is a physical Israel, with an indigenous people, a capital city called Jerusalem, and geographic borders plainly defined in Scripture. Yet there is also a spiritual Israel, with a spiritual people and a spiritual New Jerusalem. Spiritual Israel, the church, may enjoy the blessings of physical Israel, but it does not replace physical Israel in God's plan for the ages.

This distinction is clearly stated in Isaiah 40:1: "'Comfort, yes, comfort My people!' / Says your God." Take a close look at the formal English. Who is being addressed? It is obvious that one group is being comforted and another is offering comfort.

Logic tells us we cannot be comforting and comforted at the same time. The people being comforted in this verse are "My people," or the Jewish people. The next verse makes this plain: "Speak comfort to Jerusalem, and cry out to her, / That her warfare is ended, / That her iniquity is pardoned" (Isa. 40:2).

The people doing the comforting is spiritual Israel, the church.

The Bible concept of two Israels, one physical and the other spiritual, is validated by God's revelation to Abraham concerning his seed. God showed Abraham his spiritual seed in Genesis 22:17: "Blessing I will bless you, and multiplying I will multiply your descendants as the stars of the heaven and as the sand which is on the seashore."

God mentions two separate and distinct elements: stars of the heaven and sand of the seashore.

The "stars of the heaven" represent the church, or spiritual Israel. Stars, as light, rule the darkness, which is the commission of the church. Jesus said, "You are the light of the world" (Matt. 5:14). Jesus is called "the Bright and Morning Star" (Rev. 22:16). Daniel 12:3 tells us that "Those who are wise shall shine / Like the brightness of the firmament, / And those who turn many to righteousness / Like the stars forever and ever." A star gave guidance and led wise men to the house in Bethlehem where Jesus was.

Stars are heavenly, not earthly. They represent the church, spiritual Israel.

The "sand of the seashore," on the other hand, is earthly and represents an earthly kingdom with a literal Jerusalem as the capital city.

Both stars and sand exist at the same time, and neither ever replaces the other. Just so, the nation of Israel and spiritual Israel, the church, exist at the same time and do not replace each other. In Revelation 7:4–8, physical Israel is alive and well, represented by twelve tribes and 144,000 who were sealed by God to preach the gospel during the Great Tribulation.

In 1948 Israel was reborn, and the Seed of Abraham returned to the Promised Land to become one of the world's most dynamic nations. Replaced? Never. Revived? Yes!

According to John the Revelator, Israel is still thriving during the Tribulation when the church is in heaven. John writes: "And I heard the number of those who were sealed. One hundred and forty-four thousand of all the tribes of the children of Israel were sealed" (Rev. 7:4).

The two Israels will merge together on the day when the Messiah literally enters the physical city of Jerusalem. The prophet Zechariah describes the coming of the Messiah: "And I will pour on the house of David and on the inhabitants of

Jerusalem the Spirit of grace and supplication," wrote the prophet, "then they will look on Me whom they pierced. Yes, they will mourn for Him as one mourns for his only son, and grieve for Him as one grieves for a firstborn" (12:10).

Unless we grasp the concept of two Israels peacefully coexisting and never replacing each other, we will fall into the false doctrine of past centuries. The tragedy is that our ignorance ultimately injures Israel and the Jewish people and invites the wrath of God upon us and our descendants.

Boycott Israel?

American replacement theologians are preaching, "If Christians will quit supporting Israel and economically boycott the Christ-rejecting Jews, the Jews will accept Jesus Christ."[3]

An economic boycott of national Israel is not going to hasten the day Jews convert and become spiritual Israel. This anti-Semitic logic defies and ignores both history and the Bible.

The Jews were economically attacked by crusaders who murdered, raped, and robbed them in the name of God. They didn't accept Christ after that tragedy. The Jews of the Spanish Inquisition were tortured and terrorized as the church extorted their wealth. They did not become Christians, even when they were forced to surrender their children to be raised by Gentile neighbors because they were under death sentences from the church.

Economically, Adolf Hitler brought the Jews to their knees by forbidding them to have jobs. He destroyed their places of business in the infamous Night of Broken Glass, and then fined them billions of deutsche marks to repair the damage his Nazi hoodlums had inflicted. They did not become Christians even when he systematically slaughtered six million of them. As Jews walked to the gas chamber they sang "Hatkivah," not "Amazing Grace."

The Bible says:

- "And so all Israel will be saved" (Rom. 11:26).
- Israel will welcome the Messiah (see Zech. 12:10).
- Israel will come to repentance (see Rom. 11:27).

When will Israel welcome its Messiah? Look at Romans 11:25: "For I do not desire, brethren," Paul writes, "that you should be ignorant of this mystery, lest you should be wise in your own opinion, that blindness in part has happened to Israel until the fullness of the Gentiles has come in." The word translated *fullness* is the Greek word *pleroma*. The word refers not to a numerical capacity, but to a sense of *completeness*.

"The completion of the mission to the Gentiles will result in, or lead to, Israel's 'fullness' or 'completion' (Rom. 11:12), her 'acceptance' (Rom. 11:15)," write scholars Walter C. Kaiser Jr., Peter H. Davids, F. F. Bruce, and Manfred T. Brauch in *Hard Sayings of the Bible*. "Paul proclaims this future realization of God's intention as 'a mystery' (Rom. 11:25). . . . The most instructive parallel to this text—which envisions the grafting of both Gentile and Jew into the same olive tree—is Ephesians 3:3–6, where Paul says that the content of the 'mystery of Christ' is the inclusion of the Gentiles as fellow heirs of the promise with Jews in the new community of Christ's body."[4]

Bible scholars agree that Paul's statement that "all Israel will be saved" means Israel "as a whole," not every single individual. Just as the phrase "the fullness of the Gentiles" (Rom. 11:25) does not mean every single Gentile will accept

Jesus as Messiah, even so not every single child of Israel will place his or her faith in the Christ. But when the "fullness of the Gentiles" has come, that is, when the Gentiles' time of grace is completed, then God will remove their blindness (Rom. 11:10) to the identity of Messiah and "all Israel will be saved" (Rom. 11:26).

"What is also clear from the whole thrust of the discussion in Romans 9—11," write the aforementioned scholars, "is that God's purposes for the salvation of Israel will be realized in no other way and by no other means than through the preaching of the gospel and the response of faith."[5]

By faithfully sharing the gospel, you may lead a Jewish friend to Christ, but the idea that the Jews of the world are going to convert and storm the doors of Christian churches is a delusion born of ignorance. After 2,000 years of a loveless, anti-Semitic Christianity that has saturated the soil of the earth with Jewish blood, the Jews are not about to convert en masse.

Those who target Jews for conversion quoting Romans 1:16 ("For I am not ashamed of the gospel of Christ, for it is the power of God to salvation for everyone who believes, for the Jew first and also for the Greek") twist the Scripture. The subject of Romans 1:16 is *the gospel*. Paul's words "to the Jew first," do not refer to priority. His words are a statement of *sequence,* not *preference*. The gospel came to the Jewish people first (see Rom. 3:2), and then to the Gentiles. God is not a respecter of persons.

Where is the Christianity that says, "Love your neighbor as you love yourself"? Where is the Christianity that says, "Love suffers long and is kind; love does not envy"? Where are the Christians who practice "Love one another as I have loved you"? Where is the Christianity, born of the blood of Jesus of Nazareth, who said, "In as much as you have done it unto the least of these *My brethren* [the Jews], you have done it unto Me"?

Jews and Judaism have not lost their credibility; but all too often a loveless Christianity has abandoned the law of love only to become sounding brass and clanging cymbals. Until the Lord's return, why should any Jew want to follow a Messiah whose followers feel compelled to hate, murder, rob, and rape while they brazenly proclaim, "We are the singular people of God"?

If Replaced, Why Reborn?

For 1,800 years, the church fathers ranted that the church is the new Israel. To prove that God had turned His back on the Jews, they pointed to the wandering, tormented Jews of the Diaspora, saying, "If God is with them, why has this homelessness befallen them?"

They forget that for the most part European Jews were living in states controlled by the Church of Rome. They were existing without rights, without property, without legal redress, and without human dignity. The medieval church created its own self-fulfilling prophecy.

Replacement theologians ignore a fundamental fact in the biblical text. When God removes or destroys something, you never hear from it again. Like Sodom and Gomorrah, which were so thoroughly destroyed that archaeologists can't even find the ashes of those cities, it is twice dead, plucked up by the roots and cast over the wall to be burned and forever forgotten. If the church fathers were correct and Israel were indeed replaced, she should have vanished like snow in the desert sun. By all rights, she should have disappeared. But she didn't.

On May 15, 1948, a theological earthquake leveled replacement theology when the State of Israel was reborn after 2,000 years of wandering. From the four corners of the earth, the Seed of Abraham returned to the land of their fathers. They arose from their Gentile "graves" (Ezek. 37:12) speaking sixty different languages, and they founded a nation that has become a superpower in forty years. Far from passing away, the State of Israel is building, growing, inventing, and developing. The desert is indeed blooming like a rose, just as Isaiah the prophet promised (35:1).

You can't avoid the central issue. If God was finished with the Jews and Israel, if they were really a cast-off relic of the past without divine purpose or destiny, why did He allow the State to be miraculously renewed? If replaced, why reborn?

The resurrection of God's chosen people is living prophetic proof that Israel has not been replaced. They were reborn in a day (Isa. 66:8) to form the State of Israel that shall endure until the coming of Messiah.

If Israel as a nation had not been reborn, if the Jews had not returned to the land, if the cities of Israel had not been rebuilt, if Judea and Samaria (the West Bank) had not been occupied, if the trees the Turks cut down had not been replanted, if the agricultural accomplishments of Israel had not been miraculous, there would be a valid reason to doubt that the Word of God is true. However, in light of the above-mentioned miracles, none can doubt the absolute accuracy of the prophetic Scriptures concerning the rebirth and restoration of the Jewish state.

Listen to God's Word as His prophets declare His intention for the Jews to inhabit Israel. Isaiah wrote:

Fear not, for I am with you;
I will bring your descendants from the east,
And gather you from the west;
I will say to the north, "Give them up!"

And to the south, "Do not keep them back!"
Bring My sons from afar,
And My daughters from the ends of the earth (43:5–6).

And the ransomed of the LORD shall return,
And come to Zion with singing,
With everlasting joy on their heads.
They shall obtain joy and gladness,
And sorrow and sighing shall flee away (35:10).

And they shall rebuild the old ruins,
They shall raise up the former desolations,
And they shall repair the ruined cities,
The desolations of many generations (61:4).

Who confirms the word of His servant,
And performs the counsel of His messengers;
Who says to Jerusalem, "You shall be inhabited,"
To the cities of Judah, "You shall be built,"
And I will raise up her waste places (44:26).

Ezekiel speaks:

"As I live," says the Lord GOD, "surely with a mighty
hand, with an outstretched arm, and with fury poured
out, I will rule over you. I will bring you out from the
peoples and gather you out of the countries where you
are scattered, with a mighty hand, with an outstretched
arm, and with fury poured out. . . . For on My holy
mountain, on the mountain height of Israel," says the
Lord GOD, "there all the house of Israel, all of them in
the land, shall serve Me; there I will accept them, and
there I will require your offerings and the firstfruits of
your sacrifices, together with all your holy things. I will
accept you as a sweet aroma when I bring you out from
the peoples and gather you out of the countries where
you have been scattered; and I will be hallowed in you

before the Gentiles. Then you shall know that I am the LORD, when I bring you into the land of Israel, into the country for which I raised My hand in an oath to give to your fathers" (20:33–34, 40–42).

"And they shall no longer be a prey for the nations, nor shall beasts of the land devour them; but they shall dwell safely, and no one shall make them afraid. I will raise up for them a garden of renown, and they shall no longer be consumed with hunger in the land, nor bear the shame of the Gentiles anymore. Thus they shall know that I, the LORD their God, am with them, and they, the house of Israel, are My people," says the Lord GOD (34:28–30).

Therefore say, "Thus says the Lord GOD: 'I will gather you from the peoples, assemble you from the countries where you have been scattered, and I will give you the land of Israel.' And they will go there, and they will take away all its detestable things and all its abominations from there. Then I will give them one heart, and I will put a new spirit within them" (11:17–19).

Jeremiah speaks:

Behold, I will bring back the captivity of Jacob's tents,
And have mercy on his dwelling places;
The city shall be built upon its own mound,
And the palace shall remain according to its own plan (30:18).

Hear the word of the LORD, O nations,
And declare it in the isles afar off, and say,
"He who scattered Israel will gather him,
And keep him as a shepherd does his flock."
For the LORD has redeemed Jacob,
And ransomed him from the hand of one stronger than he.
Therefore they shall come and sing in the height of Zion,

Streaming to the goodness of the LORD—
For wheat and new wine and oil,
For the young of the flock and the herd;
Their souls shall be like a well-watered garden,
And they shall sorrow no more at all (31:10–12).

> "For behold, the days are coming," says the LORD,
> "that I will bring back from captivity My people Israel
> and Judah," says the LORD. "And I will cause them to
> return to the land that I gave to their fathers, and they
> shall possess it. . . .
> "Therefore do not fear, O My servant Jacob,"
>   says the LORD,
> "Nor be dismayed, O Israel;
> For behold, I will save you from afar,
> And your seed from the land of their captivity.
> Jacob shall return, have rest and be quiet,
> And no one shall make him afraid.
> For I am with you," says the LORD, "to save you;
> Though I make a full end of all nations where I
>   have scattered you" (30:3, 10–11).

David speaks:

When the LORD brought back the captivity of Zion,
We were like those who dream.
Then our mouth was filled with laughter,
And our tongue with singing.
Then they said among the nations,
"The LORD has done great things for them" (Ps. 126:1–2).

Oh, give thanks to the LORD, for He is good!
For His mercy endures forever.
Let the redeemed of the LORD say so,
Whom He has redeemed from the hand of the enemy,
And gathered out of the lands,

From the east and from the west,
From the north and from the south (Ps. 107:1–3).

Zechariah testifies of things to come:

> So the angel who spoke with me said to me, "Pro-
> claim, saying, 'Thus says the LORD of hosts:
> "I am zealous for Jerusalem
> And for Zion with great zeal.
> I am exceedingly angry with the nations at ease;
> For I was a little angry,
> And they helped—but with evil intent."
> 'Therefore thus says the LORD:
> "I am returning to Jerusalem with mercy;
> My house shall be built in it," says the LORD of
> hosts,
> "And a surveyor's line shall be stretched out over
> Jerusalem."'
> Again proclaim, saying, 'Thus says the LORD of
> hosts:
> "My cities shall again spread out through prosperity;
> The LORD will again comfort Zion,
> And will again choose Jerusalem""" (1:14–17).

The Old Testament prophets are clear and united in their opinions—replacement theology is completely wrong, misguided, deceived, ill conceived, and incorrect. The Jews have not been replaced, for they will return to Jerusalem, the city of God, and the God of Abraham, Isaac, and Jacob will be their God.

Jesus Did Not Support Replacement Theology

Jesus was the greatest teacher of the ages. He gave us three chapters (Matt. 24, Mark 13, and Luke 21) that are prophetic and present the chronological events of the future from His time until His second coming. In Matthew 24:3, His disciples asked Jesus three questions:

1. *When shall these things be?* This question referred to the destruction of the temple. Jesus answered in Luke 21:20, "When you see Jerusalem surrounded by armies, then know that its desolation is near." This prediction was fulfilled in A.D. 70 when the Roman general Titus destroyed Jerusalem.

2. *And what will be the sign of Your coming?*

3. *And of the end of the age?* In spite of the kingdom now theology (whose adherents believe the church will be so victorious that we will usher in the millennial age), this world is coming to an end. In Galatians 1:4, Paul wrote that Christ "gave Himself for our sins, that He might *deliver us* from this present evil age, according to the will of our God and Father" (italics mine).

There is not a single hint in one of these passages supporting replacement theology. Paul did not mention the demise of the Jewish nation, nor did Jesus.

Let's look at Matthew 24:15–18, where Jesus described the great period of tribulation that will come upon the earth. This verse assumes that Israel is living in its homeland and in control of the city of Jerusalem. "Therefore," said Jesus, "when you see the 'abomination of desolation,' spoken of by Daniel the prophet, standing in the holy place . . . then let those who are in Judea flee to the mountains. Let him who is on the housetop not go down to take anything out of his house. And let him who is in the field not go back to get his clothes."

The "holy place" Jesus mentioned is the temple in Jerusalem. The Jews are in control of the temple at this time right before the Tribulation. How could they control the temple without being in control of Jerusalem? How could they be in control of Jerusalem if they were replaced?

"Let those who are in Judea flee to the mountains," Jesus said. Judea is what the media now call the West Bank. Jesus' statement assumes that in the last days the Jews would be living on the West Bank. In the next several verses, Jesus describes a general evacuation of the population in and around Jerusalem because of a pending military attack.

When this military attack comes, warned Jesus, don't go to Jerusalem for safety. You will have only a few minutes to save your life. Flee to the mountains outside Jerusalem as a matter of civil defense. Jesus continues, "Let him who is on the housetop not go down to take anything out of his house. And let him who is in the field not go back to get his clothes."

The rooftops in Jerusalem, both now and in Jesus' time, are flat. People store things on the roof and sometimes even sleep there. There is usually an outside stairway leading to the ground. When this attack comes, Jesus warned, don't worry about saving anything in the house, just run for your life. And if you are in the fields, laboring in your work clothes, don't run back to the house to change.

Jesus continues: "But woe to those who are pregnant and to those who are nursing babies in those days! And pray that your flight may not be in winter or on the Sabbath. For then there will be great tribulation, such as has not been since the beginning of the world until this time, no, nor ever shall be" (Matt. 24:19–21).

Why woe to those who are pregnant and with nursing babies? Why pray that your escape be not in winter or on the Sabbath? Because an escape would be much more difficult. This verse again indicates that the religious Jews are in control of an Israeli government where the laws of the Sabbath are being strictly enforced.

I don't know if you've had the opportunity to travel in Israel on the Sabbath, but I can assure you that everything shuts down on Saturday. There is no transportation. Even the elevators in the hotels and high-rise apartments stop on every floor automatically. If an Arab missile with a nuclear warhead or poison gas struck Jerusalem on the Sabbath, the attack would result in mass destruction.

Jesus confirms that the Jews are back in Israel in Matthew 24:22 when He says, "And unless those days were short-ened, no flesh would be saved; but for the elect's sake those days will be shortened."

"The elect" are the Jewish people. If Jesus and the prophets were convinced that Israel would return to the land, and if they were certain Israel had not been cast aside or replaced in the economy of God, how is it that America's replacement theologians have come up with a different idea? Did it spring from narcissism? Anti-Semitism?

Replacement Theology Is Idolatry

Replacement theology violates the Ten Commandments. First Samuel 15:23 tells us, "For rebellion is as the sin of witchcraft, / And stubbornness is as iniquity and idolatry."

This verse says two things: (1) Rebellion equals witchcraft and (2) stubbornness equals idolatry. Who is a stubborn person? People who refuse to change their ideas even when they are in direct conflict with God's Word are the worst kind of stubborn. These people idolize their opinions and are soon in open rebellion against the will and Word of God.

Christians would never dream of allowing their pastor to preach with a statue of Buddha draped around his neck—that's open idolatry. But they think nothing of permitting their pastor, whose stubborn personal opinions about Israel are exactly opposite the Word of God, to lead them into dangerous deception.

Has the church replaced Israel? Not in the opinion of Jesus and the prophets of Israel. The canon of Scripture and modern history are witnesses to the fact that Israel has been reborn and will endure forever.

From the dark days of Jewish persecution in Germany, a legend has survived. According to the story, a pastor, acting on Nazi orders, looked out upon his congregation and told them, "All of you who had Jewish fathers will leave and not return."

A few worshipers rose and slipped out of the sanctuary. The pastor then said, "All of you who had Jewish mothers must go and not return."

Again, a few worshipers arose and departed. Suddenly those who remained in their pews turned pale and began to tremble with fear. The figure of Christ on the cross above the altar loosed itself and left the church.

Think about it. If Jesus Christ came to your church this Sunday morning, would the ushers let Him enter the front door? He would appear small and slender, with penetrating dark eyes, a swarthy complexion, and prominent Semitic features. He would have earlocks, hair uncut at the corners, and full beard. His shoulders would be draped with a tallit, or prayer shawl.

If Jesus identified Himself to your congregation as a Rabbi who befriended prostitutes and socialized with tax collectors and people with AIDS, would He be welcomed? If He confessed that He was hated by the government and traveled with twelve unemployed men with full beards and shoulder-length hair, could they find a seat in your pews?

If your deacons asked Him about His doctrinal positions and He responded, "I believe in baptism by immersion, casting out demons, and healing the sick," would they let Him stand behind your pulpit?

If He commanded your wealthiest church members to sell all they had to give to the poor, if He entered your beautiful church gym and turned over the bingo tables shouting, "My house shall be called a house of prayer," would you call the police?

The simple truth is this. After 2,000 years of anti-Semitic teaching and preaching, we have lost sight of the Jewishness of our Hebrew Savior. But He was born to Jewish parents, His ancestors were Jewish, He was raised in the Jewish tradition, He lived and worshiped as a Jew, He died as a Jew, and He will return as a Jew. When you kneel tonight to pray, the One who hears you is a Rabbi named Jesus of Nazareth.

PART II

THE
PROPHECIES
OF
JERUSALEM

CHAPTER 7

JERUSALEM THE GOLDEN

There is Israel, for us at least. What no other gen-
eration had, we have. We have Israel in spite of all
the dangers, the threats and the wars, we have Israel.
We can go to Jerusalem. Generations and genera-
tions could not and we can.
—Elie Wiesel, Romanian-born American writer[1]

We have discussed the *people* of Jerusalem—
a nation that wandered homeless for thousands of years, a
nation persecuted without valid cause even in the name of
Christ. We've seen how God's divine principle of blessing
and cursing Israel has been graphically demonstrated in the
lives of individuals and political powers. We've learned that
Israel has not been replaced or removed from God's covenant
and plan. Now we will see how *prophecies* regarding the
Seed of Abraham will affect the future of all men and every
nation on earth.

Focal Point of the Past and Future: Jerusalem

Medieval mapmakers (quite rightfully, in my opinion) placed beautiful Jerusalem at the center of the world. They understood what Bible scholars have known for years—Jerusalem is the center of the universe, the focal point of things to come and things in the past.

The ancient city of Jerusalem is the heart and soul of the nation of Israel. While other cities around the world are known for their commerce, their size, their wealth, or their outstanding architecture, Jerusalem ascends to the pinnacle of world prominence with accolades that can be given to no other city on earth. Jerusalem is the chosen city of God:

> I [God] have chosen Jerusalem, that My name may be there. . . . For now I have chosen and sanctified this house [the temple], that My name may be there forever; and My eyes and My heart will be there perpetually. . . . In this house and in Jerusalem, which I have chosen out of all the tribes of Israel, I will put My name forever (2 Chron. 6:6; 7:16; 33:7).

Jerusalem is a small city by many standards. With a population of just over a half million, it is certainly not the most populous city in the world. And yet it dominates head-lines of newspapers and is known as the Holy City to Muslims, Christians, and Jews.

History of the Holy City

Jerusalem, whose very dust is adored in Scripture, was first settled by Canaanites in the twentieth century B.C. Though only a little larger than twelve acres in size, the city was naturally well defended and had at its base one of the most abundant springs in the area. By about 1,000 years before Christ, Jerusalem was inhabited by Jebusites, a group of people related to the Hittites of the Old Testament.

By the time David was anointed king of Israel in the last decade of the eleventh century B.C., the nation of Israel needed a strong central capitol. David searched for a location among the tribes, and in 1004 B.C. he conquered a Jebusite city and made it his capitol.

David's passion for the Holy City is evident as that poet and warrior statesman of Israel wrote,

> If I forget you, O Jerusalem,
> Let my right hand forget its skill!
> If I do not remember you,
> Let my tongue cling to the roof of my mouth—
> If I do not exalt Jerusalem
> Above my chief joy (Ps. 137:5–6).

As you may recall, David was a musician. With his right hand he played the harp and sang the songs of Israel with such power that the demons of King Saul were silenced. If David's tongue were frozen to the roof of his mouth and his right hand could no longer play, his life as a musician would be over.

David's message was simple. If he were to forget Jerusalem, his life would have no meaning. If Jerusalem was not the source of his deepest joy, he felt there was no need to exist. He saw Jerusalem as the Holy City, the place God and God's people called home.

In Jerusalem, David's son Solomon built his magnificent and ornate temple.

In Jerusalem, Jeremiah and Isaiah uttered thoughts that molded the spiritual foundations of half the human race.

In Jerusalem, Jesus Christ of Nazareth wept on the Mount of Olives hours before His crucifixion. "O Jerusalem, Jerusalem," He prayed, "the one who kills the prophets and stones those who are sent to her! How often I wanted to gather your children together, as a hen gathers her chicks under her wings, but you were not willing!" (Matt. 23:37).

In A.D. 70 Titus sent his troops into Jerusalem and slaughtered the Jews until their blood literally streamed down the streets. The Romans completely sacked the city and destroyed most of the second temple, which had been completed only six years before. The Romans continued the slaughter of the Jews of Jerusalem. In A.D. 135 a Jewish Diaspora began as Hadrian, a second-century Roman emperor, barred Jews from Jerusalem and had survivors of the massacre dispersed across the Roman Empire. Many fleeing Jews escaped to Mediterranean ports only to be sold into slavery.

The crusaders, marching under the sign of the cross, stormed into Jerusalem in 1099. Again the streets of the city ran with blood as the crusaders slaughtered over 40,000 people and set fire to mosques and synagogues. As screams for mercy rose from the lips of tortured Jews inside their synagogues, the crusaders lustily sang hymns of praise to God.

Jerusalem means "city of peace," but it has known more war, more bloodshed, more tears, and more terror than any other city on earth. It has been conquered and reconquered thirty-eight times by Babylonians, Greeks, Romans, crusaders, and Ottomans, yet it stands united and indivisible.

Only the mighty hand of God could have preserved Jerusalem from its birth under King David until the stunning moment in the 1967 Six-Day War when Jewish soldiers broke through the Jordanian front and prayed together at the Western Wall. After almost 2,000 years, the ancient city of Jerusalem once again was restored into Jewish hands through a supernatural victory of the Israeli army.

But Jerusalem is the city that symbolizes God's power to protect His people:

> Those who trust in the LORD
> Are like Mount Zion,
> Which cannot be moved, but abides forever.
> As the mountains surround Jerusalem,
> So the LORD surrounds His people
> From this time forth and forever (Ps. 125:1–2).

God will preserve Jerusalem. It is *His* Holy City.

Jerusalem Today

What's happening in Jerusalem today? Jerusalem the Golden is caught in a supernatural crossfire. Trading land for peace will not bring peace. Making Jerusalem an international city under the pope will not bring peace. Giving Yasser Arafat and the PLO part of Jerusalem to establish a Palestinian city will not bring peace.

The enemies of Israel and of the Jewish people will not be satisfied until they control Jerusalem. Christians and Jews, let us stand united and indivisible on this issue: There can be no compromise regarding the city of Jerusalem, not now, not ever. We are racing toward the end of time, and Israel lies in the eye of the storm.

My newspaper's morning headlines recently screamed THIRTY-ONE PALESTINIANS SHOT AS HEBRON RIOTS RAGE. Jerusalem radio news programs frequently warn that terrorists may strike soon. The front page of the *Jerusalem Post*'s international edition declares, ISRAELI PRIME MINISTER REJECTS

MAKE-BELIEVE PEACE. As I write this, Islamic suicide bombers have just invaded the peaceful Mahaneh Yehuda market, leaving 16 dead and 176 innocent people wounded.

In recent days on the streets of Tel Aviv, a HAMAS (Islamic Resistance Movement) suicide bomber killed twenty-two and wounded nearly four dozen. The bomb he carried was so powerful that it shredded a bus. Bits of human hair and flesh had to be scraped off nearby walls.

Bloody street battles are fought weekly in West Bank cities. Stark images of mourners picking up rocks after a funeral and charging Israeli soldiers leap from the pages of *Time* and *Newsweek*. Rubber bullets and flying rocks in Ramallah are a testimonial that men cry "Peace, peace," but there is no peace. Anyone who thinks peace is coming to the city of Jerusalem and the Middle East is living in a world of illusion.

What is the meaning behind these signs of the times? The end of the world as we know it is drawing near. And although the action is now in Israel, the future and destiny of the entire planet hang in the balance.

God has made it possible to know the future through Bible prophecy. My years of studying the writings of the ancient Bible prophets have given me a panoramic view, not only of what is ahead, but how it will all unfold. The guidelines for tomorrow are available to us today.

God Remembers

God's megaphones came in human form. He chose righteous men to preach His message and proclaim prophecy. Zechariah was such a man. Born of priestly lineage, Zechariah lived during one of the most significant periods of upheaval in the saga of Israel. Struggling exiles returning from Babylon rebuilt the blackened ruins of

Jerusalem and the temple. Zechariah knew God was getting ready to do a great thing; however, in writing to encourage the weary laborers, he also left us with vital clues to understand God's everlasting plan.

Zekar-yah, the prophet's name in Hebrew, means "God remembers." In fact, Zechariah's theme is that Israel will be blessed precisely because God remembers the covenants and agreements He made with the patriarchs. No one was better equipped to explore the mind of God than this walking symbol of the faithful memory of Almighty God.

Zechariah wasn't surprised when he got the message about the future. Another prophet had already described what lay ahead for Israel. Isaiah foresaw the coming fall and conquest of the Hebrews by Babylonian hordes. Isaiah gave Zechariah his first inkling of an astonishing divine surprise awaiting Jerusalem and the Jews.

Through Isaiah, God promised the complete restoration of Jerusalem. He wrote, "I have set watchmen on your walls, O Jerusalem; / They shall never hold their peace day or night. / You who make mention of the LORD, do not keep silent, / And give Him no rest till He establishes / And till He makes Jerusalem a praise in the earth" (62:6–7).

The future of the Holy City is the centerpiece of God's blueprint for history. God will reorder, restore, redouble, redistribute, reclaim, remove, renovate, recycle, recommit, and redeem until Jerusalem has become the crowning gem of all the cities on earth.

Why You Should Study Prophecy

How can you sift the truth from the nonsense when you pick up a newspaper and read about Israel? You must pay careful attention to what God has already said about the future of Jerusalem and Israel. Prophecy is the divine security system to alert us ahead of time. Let me give you four reasons to study what God said centuries ago through His prophets:

1. *Prophecy reveals the purposes of God.* God wants the world to know what's coming. The heavenly Father desires to reveal Himself and His motives. God's way comes through God's Word. Holy Scripture is His vehicle for communication. When the wickedness of Sodom and Gomorrah reached intolerable proportions, God went first to Abraham and told him He was going to destroy the cities of Sodom and Gomorrah (Gen. 18). This was a revelation of the purpose of God through predictive prophecy.

   In Genesis 18:17–18 we read, "And the LORD said, 'Shall I hide from Abraham what I am doing, since Abraham shall surely become a great and mighty nation, and all the nations of the earth shall be blessed in him?'" God divulged the future to Abraham. Otherwise Abraham might have asked himself, "Why did God do that? What was God's purpose in the destruction of every person in those two cities?"

   God revealed His purpose to Abraham so that when the destruction took place Abraham would understand that God was holy and that He would not tolerate the sins of Sodom and Gomorrah.

   As we study prophecy we understand the economic and political events in Europe that will bring the Antichrist to power; we understand Russia and its desire to once again become a military superpower by conquering Israel; we understand the global rush for a one-world currency, religion, and government. Prophecy reveals the purposes of God and demonstrates beyond any doubt that God knows the end from the beginning and that He is orchestrating the events on earth to fulfill His exact purposes.

2. *Prophecy demonstrates God's ability to know the future.* Powerful generals and clever politicians think they have the power and capacity to wield total authority and create empires, yet God is the One who raises up and puts down whom He chooses. Nations rise and fall by His design. Well before earthly coronations, the Almighty chooses who sits on the throne of each individual nation.

The second chapter of the book of Daniel contains one of the most remarkable visions God ever gave to humanity. Nebuchadnezzar thought of himself as the absolute emperor of the world, but God sent the king a particularly worrisome dream. Nebuchadnezzar dreamed of a great image made of gold, silver, bronze, and iron, with clay feet. In his dream, a massive boulder suddenly smashed into the statue, turning it into a mountain of rubble that filled the entire earth.

Nebuchadnezzar was troubled. In his heart of hearts he knew a force far greater than himself was the true power behind his throne. The king longed to understand the meaning of his dreadful dream, but when he awoke, only the troubled feelings remained—he had completely forgotten the details.

Daniel, who was in service to the Babylonian king, seized this opportunity to tell the king that God alone can reveal such mysteries because He alone knows the future. Daniel's inspired interpretation revealed the dream and completely explained each element of it.

The statue's golden head represented Nebuchadnezzar, and the other elements represented other kingdoms that would soon follow his. The Medes and the

Persians, symbolized by the image's breastplate of silver, were waiting in the wings. Their kingdoms were displaced by Alexander the Great of Greece, the statue's loins of brass. Alexander's kingdom fell to the Roman Empire, the strong and mighty domain, which eventually divided into Eastern and Western empires.

Daniel noted that the lower his inner eye descended over the image, the weaker the materials became. The statue's feet were composed of iron and clay, two materials that will not blend with each other. The "partly strong and partly broken" kingdom of Rome did weaken as it aged, until it finally divided into ten toes, or ten kingdoms.

Those ten toes, or kingdoms, will be some sort of European federation in the last days, and from this ten-member confederacy a "man of peace" will rise to take the world stage. He will be a masterful orator, and with his genius he will lead the world to a superficial, temporary prosperity.

He is the Antichrist. He will make Hitler look like a choirboy. He will sign a seven-year peace treaty with Israel and break it after three and a half years. At that time he will set himself up to be worshiped in the city of Jerusalem. He will want Jerusalem for his holy city, and he will try to exterminate every Jew in Israel.

But Nebuchadnezzar's dream did not end with the ten toes. The Babylonian king saw a rock "cut without hands" demolish the great image, and that indestructible stone was Jesus Christ. At His second coming, the world's Messiah will crush His adversaries and establish His Millennial Kingdom, the 1,000-year reign of Christ.

As he interpreted, Daniel reminded the king of the dream and revealed its hidden mystery. The king was astonished and cried out in awe, "Truly your God is the God of gods, the Lord of kings, and a revealer of secrets, since you could reveal this secret"(Dan. 2:47). Nebuchadnezzar had just become a believer in Bible prophecy. The king understood that God knows.

3. *Prophecy is absolutely accurate.* The apostle Peter read the writings of Zechariah, Isaiah, Daniel, and the other prophets. He had been an eyewitness to their fulfillment in the coming of Jesus Christ. Reflecting on the astonishing accuracy of the prophets, he wrote this summation:

> We have the prophetic word confirmed, which you do well to heed as a light that shines in a dark place, until the day dawns and the morning star rises in your hearts; knowing this first, that no prophecy of Scripture is of any private interpretation, for prophecy never came by the will of man, but holy men of God spoke as they were moved by the Holy Spirit (2 Peter 1:19–21).

Peter wanted every Christian to know that Jehovah not only speaks, but is 100 percent correct in what He says. While Peter had been an eyewitness to Jesus' ministry and resurrection, he knew prophecy was even more accurate than an eyewitness account. The human eye and ear are never completely trustworthy because distortions can creep in. But when God speaks, the communication is totally and completely perfect. You can bet your eternal soul on the accuracy of Bible prophecy.

4. *Prophecy validates the authority of God's Word.* Cults delight in making strange and esoteric statements. Although they love to tickle people's ears with fanciful ideas, they are strangely silent about the future. The Bible, however, is filled with specifics about tomorrow.

Consider the absolute accuracy concerning the life of Christ:

- The time of Jesus' birth is described in Daniel 9.
- The fact of Jesus' virgin birth is detailed in Isaiah 7:14.
- The place of Jesus' birth is forecast in Micah 5:2.
- The technicalities of His death are depicted in Psalm 22 and Isaiah 53.
- The Resurrection is prophesied in Psalm 16:10.

This is only a partial listing; I could list over six dozen references to prophecies about the Messiah that were fulfilled in Jesus Christ. In fact, the odds of those prophecies pointing to anyone other than Jesus are staggering.

One mathematician put his pencil to the problem and derived an extraordinary conclusion. The odds of all the Bible prophecies coming true in the life of one person—Jesus—is one in 87 followed by 93 zeroes!

CHAPTER 8

WINDS OF WAR
OVER JERUSALEM

Think back with me, if you will, to September 13, 1993. Israeli prime minister Yitzhak Rabin stood in the White House Rose Garden with Yasser Arafat. President Bill Clinton stood between these two men, eager to announce that Rabin and Arafat had, the previous day, signed the West Bank accord. At that signing, Rabin declared that the land flowing with milk and honey should not become a land flowing with blood and tears. In a speech delivered only a few days before, Rabin had said, "We, the soldiers who have returned from battles stained with blood; we who have seen our relatives and friends killed before our eyes; we who have attended their funerals and cannot look in the eyes of their parents; we who have come from a land where parents bury their children; we who have fought against you, the Palestinians—we say to you today, in a loud and a clear voice: enough of blood and tears. Enough."

That was a desperate and sincere cry from the soul of a warrior, but two years later, in Jerusalem, Rabin was assassinated. Blood and tears flowed again, and the leaders of the world stood at his graveside and mourned the man who had tried to bring peace to his country and failed.

Why will there be no peace in that troubled part of the world? Because an ancient rivalry exists, one that goes back all the way to Abraham.

To honor Abraham for his faith and obedience, God dispatched an angel to tell Abraham that he would be the father of a great nation: "And behold, the word of the LORD came to him, saying, . . . 'One who will come from your own body shall be your heir.' Then He brought him outside and said, 'Look now toward heaven, and count the stars if you are able to number them.' And He said to him, 'So shall your descendants be'" (Gen. 15:4–5).

Abraham was more than a little surprised at this revelation because his wife was already postmenopausal and had never borne a child. Sarah, Abraham's wife, trying to help God out a bit, asked Abraham to visit the tent of her Egyptian maid, Hagar, and have a child with her—not an unusual practice in those days. Abraham said, "Sounds like God's will to me, Sarah. 'Bye."

So Abraham slept with Hagar, and Ishmael was born. Later, just as God had foretold, Sarah did conceive and gave birth to a miracle baby, Isaac, the son of laughter. The people of Israel, the Jews, are descended from Isaac; the Arabs are descended from Ishmael.

God did honor Ishmael—He promised that Ishmael would be fruitful, the father of twelve rulers, and a great nation. But in His sovereignty, God established His covenant with Isaac, the child of promise. The title to the Promised Land of Israel passed from Abraham to Isaac and then to Jacob.

You can imagine that there was more than a little competition in Abraham's household. That rivalry still exists today, but on a larger scale. The conflict between Arabs and Jews goes deeper than disputes over the lands of Palestine. It is theological. It is Judaism versus Islam. Islam's theology insists that Islam triumph over everything else—that's why when you visit an Arabic city, the Islamic prayer tower is the highest point in the city.

The Muslims believe that while Jesus, Moses, David, and several other Hebrews were prophets, Muhammad was the greatest prophet. Though Muslims revere the Bible, including the Torah, the Psalms, and the Gospels, they hold that the *Al-Quran* (the Koran) is the absolute true word of God, revealed through the angel Jibraeel (Gabriel) to Muhammad. Muslims believe that Allah is God, that he has neither father nor mother, and that he has no sons.

Understand this: No matter what the Arabs say about peace, their religion demands that they defeat the Jews. Islam proclaims a theology of "triumphantism." Simply translated, Muslims believe that it is the will of God for Islam to rule the world.

Islamic law stipulates that to fulfill Muhammad's task, every "infidel domain" must be considered a territory of war. According to Moris Farhi, author of *The Last of Days,* Muslims believe there can be no peace with the Jew or the Christian or any other non-Islamic people, and that if peace must be made, only a truce is permissible—and that "for a maximum of ten years as an expedient to hone our swords, whet our blood, and strengthen our will."[1] Muhammad made physical violence an invisible yet integral part of that faith.

The point is this: The fundamentalist Muslims must destroy the Jews and rule Israel, or Muhammad is a false prophet and the Koran is not true. Such a thought is inconceivable. For that reason, the fundamentalist Muslims must attack Israel and the Jews in order to be loyal to their prophet. The strategy of Islamic Jihad is as simple as it is satanic: "Kill so many Jews that they will eventually abandon Palestine."[2]

The late imam Hasan al-Banna of the Islamic Resistance Movement, HAMAS, summed up their philosophy so well that his statement was included in their covenant: "Israel will exist and will continue to exist until Islam will obliterate it, just as it obliterated others before it."[3]

History of the Current Conflict

Let me briefly give you a concise history of the contemporary Israeli-Arab conflict. On May 14, 1948, the United Nations recognized the State of Israel. After 2,000 years, the Jews of the world had a homeland. The *next day*, five Arab armies attacked Israel. They attacked Israel full force, trying to murder the Zionist state in the birth canal.

But He who keeps Israel neither slumbers nor sleeps. God Almighty came to Israel's defense. Their survival was a divine miracle.

From this war of 1948 was born the "Palestinian refugee problem," which the media have used to brainwash the Western world for the past fifty years. This "refugee problem" was created, sustained, and manipulated by Arab leaders against their own people to portray the Jews of Israel as heartless. It proved to be effective.

In her book *From Time Immemorial,* historian Joan Peters charts in painstaking detail, with irrefutable documentation, that just before the war of 1948 began, Arab leaders told the Palestinians to leave their homes. "As soon as we drive the Jews into the sea," they promised, "you can return."[4]

To the Arabs' shock and surprise, they lost the war. And soon an estimated 600,000 Palestinian refugees asked Jordan, Iran, Iraq, and Syria to let them immigrate.

But the Arab states would not let them immigrate, even though they had plenty of land and money. Even though they shared a common language, religion, and culture with these refugees, permission to immigrate was denied. Why? Because the refugees had become a lightning rod for the world media to attack Israel. "See how heartless the Jewish people are?" moaned the newspapers and reporters. "See how unreasonable Israel is? Look at those poor Arabs without homes!"

Few people know that the Israeli government, along with the United Nations, put up $150 million to resettle any Arab families who wanted to return to their homes. But those who did return were shot by the Palestine Liberation Organization. "The PLO, through intimidation and murder, has largely silenced moderate Arabs who might negotiate a peaceful resolution of the conflict."[5] That's the PLO, led by Yasser Arafat, the same man who shook Rabin's hand and promised to bring peace to Israel.

Since 1948 five brutal wars have been fought in Israel. A river of blood has been shed over control of Judea and Samaria (the West Bank), control of the Golan Heights, and control over the Holy City, Jerusalem.

The peace accord signed in 1993 will last only until Syria obtains control of the Golan Heights. From there an army can easily infiltrate the West Bank to attack Jerusalem in the ultimate holy war. What happened in the Rose Garden in 1993 was the first major birth pang of World War III. The peace process leads Israel down the road to disaster.

Here's the sequence of what will happen in the days of Jerusalem's impending darkness: Until the 1993 peace accord, we had no idea how the Arabs could possibly gain a military position strong enough to attack Israel. Now we know—it was given to them in a peace treaty. The Scud missiles Saddam Hussein launched from Iraq could next be launched from the Golan Heights. Or the attack could come from the Mediterranean Sea via missiles launched from Russian submarines sold to wealthy Arab nations. A U.S. congressman sat in my office and told me, "Pastor Hagee, when the Soviet Union collapsed, some of their nuclear weapons disappeared, and no one knows where they are!"

"For when they say, 'Peace and safety!' then sudden destruction comes upon them, as labor pains upon a pregnant woman" (1 Thess. 5:3). The prophet Ezekiel saw a vast Arab coalition of nations coming against Israel (Ezek. 38—39). These armies will cover the land like a cloud. But God says that His fury "will show in My face. For in My jealousy and in the fire of My wrath I have spoken" (Ezek. 38:18–19). God will be enraged. He gave the Promised Land to Abraham, Isaac, Jacob, and their seed forever by blood covenant, and His fury will be poured out on all who try to take it from them.

Russia Will Rebound from Its Current Malaise

Make no mistake, a reborn Russia seeking to again become a military superpower will in the near future lead a massive pan-Islamic military expedition in an attempt to conquer Israel. The prophet Ezekiel paints the portrait of the coming battle with shocking clarity. Just before the return of Jesus Christ, world powers will be divided into four great sectors:

1. The king of the North, or Russia. Moscow is directly north of Jerusalem.
2. The king of the South, which consists of Egypt and the nations south of Israel.
3. The king of the West, represented by the federated states of Europe that are now coming together under the European Union.
4. The king of the East, which is represented by the Asiatic powers lying to the east of the Euphrates River.

You may be asking, "How could the Soviet Union ever be reborn?" or "What interest would either Russia or a reborn Soviet Union have in cooperating with a military campaign against Israel?"

Russia longs to be a military superpower again. Many Russians were very proud of the empire the Soviets built during the time of Communist rule. The humiliation of losing that empire, combined with the impoverishment of its faltering economy, has left the Russian people feeling nostalgic about their past, bitter about their present, and skeptical about their future. Dictators grow in such a climate, and the winds of war sweep a nation toward military conflict.

Russia must have an unlimited supply of oil to become a military superpower. Although Russia is rich with oil reserves and other natural resources, those resources tend to be located in remote areas that are difficult to access. Therefore, it must gain control of the main source of the industrialized world's oil—the Persian Gulf.

When the Islamic nations, which constantly call for holy war to annihilate Israel, join forces with Russia, they will greatly benefit from the strength of Russia's armed forces. Russia will say to the Islamic nations, "You want Jerusalem and the temple mount as a holy site. We want the Persian Gulf oil. Let's join forces to rule the world!" Watch as in the future Russia becomes extremely congenial to all Islamic states.

What will be the result? A massive pan-Islamic military force led by Russia's command will come against Israel "like a cloud, to cover the land" (Ezek. 38:16).

A Global Confrontation

Let's read how the prophet describes the conflict to come against Jerusalem and Israel:

> Now the word of the LORD came to me, saying, "Son of man, set your face against Gog, of the land of Magog, the prince of Rosh, Meshech, and Tubal, and prophesy against him, and say, 'Thus says the Lord GOD: "Behold, I am against you, O Gog, the prince of Rosh, Meshech, and Tubal. I will turn you around, put hooks into your jaws, and lead you out, with all your army, horses, and horsemen, all splendidly clothed, a great company with bucklers and shields, all of them handling swords. Persia, Ethiopia, and Libya are with them, all of them with shield and helmet; Gomer and all its troops; the house of Togarmah from the far north and all its troops—many people are with you. Prepare yourself and be ready, you and all your companies that are gathered about you; and be a guard for them. After many days you will be visited. In the latter years you will come into the land of those brought back from the sword and gathered from many people on the mountains of Israel, which had long been desolate; they were brought out of the nations, and now all of them dwell safely. You will ascend, coming like a storm, covering the land like a cloud, you and all your troops and many

peoples with you." 'Thus says the Lord GOD: "On that day it shall come to pass that thoughts will arise in your mind, and you will make an evil plan: You will say, 'I will go up against a land of unwalled villages; I will go to a peaceful people, who dwell safely, all of them dwelling without walls, and having neither bars nor gates'—to take plunder and to take booty, to stretch out your hand against the waste places that are again inhabited, and against a people gathered from the nations, who have acquired livestock and goods, who dwell in the midst of the land. . . .

"Therefore, son of man, prophesy and say to Gog, 'Thus says the Lord GOD: "On that day when My people Israel dwell safely, will you not know it? Then you will come from your place out of the far north, you and many peoples with you, all of them riding on horses, a great company and a mighty army. You will come up against My people Israel like a cloud, to cover the land. It will be in the latter days that I will bring you against My land, so that the nations may know Me, when I am hallowed in you, O Gog, before their eyes" (Ezek. 38:1–12, 14–16).

Ezekiel makes it absolutely clear that God is talking about an attack upon Israel by its enemies. The leader of the attack is Gog, and his kingdom is Magog. *Magog* is referred to as one of the sons of Japheth in Genesis 10:2 and in 1 Chronicles 1:5. Ethnologists tell us that after the Flood, the Japhethites migrated from Asia Minor to the north, beyond the Caspian and Black Seas.

The only land north of this area is Russia!

God is specifically speaking of "the prince of Rosh, Meshech, and Tubal." Many people believe "Rosh" is related to the modern word *Russia* and that "Meshech" and "Tubal," respectively, are variations of the spelling of *Moscow* and *Tobolsk*, an area in the Ural section of Russia.

The names *Russia* or *Soviet Union* do not appear in Scripture, but this detailed description of the invader of Israel clearly fits Russia. Today, the former Soviet Union has split up into separate states—and five of them are controlled by Islamic fundamentalists. One of those states has most of the nuclear missile firepower of the former Soviet Union.

With this mighty army will come other invaders: Persia, Ethiopia, Libya, Gomer, and Togarmah. I believe when Ezekiel speaks of Persia, Ethiopia, and Libya, he is speaking of the same Iranian states that are now constantly calling for holy war to exterminate Israel. Gomer and Togarmah refer to the region now occupied by the nation of Turkey.

The Vigilant Guardian of Israel

If God created Israel by His spoken word, has sworn to defend Israel, and has chosen Jerusalem as His habitation on earth, then will He not fight against those who come against the apple of His eye?

Zechariah wrote:

Behold, the day of the LORD is coming,
And your spoil will be divided in your midst.
For I will gather all the nations to battle against Jerusalem;
The city shall be taken,
The houses rifled,
And the women ravished.
Half of the city shall go into captivity,
But the remnant of the people shall not be cut off
   from the city.
Then the LORD will go forth
And fight against those nations,
As He fights in the day of battle (14:1–3).

In the latter days, just prior to the Second Coming, the nations of the world will gather to fight against Jerusalem, and God will defend His habitation on earth.

Zechariah records, "And this shall be the plague with which the LORD will strike all the people who fought against Jerusalem: Their flesh shall dissolve while they stand on their feet, / Their eyes shall dissolve in their sockets, / And their tongues shall dissolve in their mouths" (14:12).

I believe this is Zechariah's description of a nuclear blast, which can generate 150 million degrees Fahrenheit in one-millionth of a second. That's how your tongue and your eyes can dissolve in their sockets before your corpse hits the ground. God will allow the use of nuclear weapons in this great battle against Israel, but then He will step into the fray.

When the invading army comes to cover the land "like a cloud," God says, "My fury will show in My face" (Ezek. 38:18). God Himself, the Guardian of Israel who never slumbers or sleeps, will stand up and fight from the balconies of heaven to aid the Seed of Abraham.

First, He will send a mighty earthquake so devastating it will shake the mountains and the seas, and every wall shall fall to the ground (Ezek. 38:19, 20).

Second, God will send massive confusion to the multinational fighting force, and "every man's sword will be against his brother" (Ezek. 38:21).

Third, God will open fire with His divine artillery and rain down on Israel's offenders "great hailstones, fire, and brimstone" (Ezek. 38:22).

The battle casualties will be staggering. Five out of six enemy troops that attack Israel in this Russian-led pan-Islamic force will die. It will take seven months to bury the dead (Ezek. 39:12). It will take seven years to burn the implements of war (Ezek. 39:9).

Why does God slaughter the armies that invade Israel? Ezekiel gives the answer: "So I will make My holy name known in the midst of My people Israel, and I will not let them profane My holy name anymore. Then the nations shall know that I am the LORD, the Holy One in Israel. . . . So the house of Israel shall know that I am the LORD their God from that day forward" (Ezek. 39:7, 22).

Israel is the only nation created by a sovereign act of God, and He has sworn by His holiness to defend Jerusalem, His Holy City. If God created and defends Israel, those nations that fight against it fight against God.

But how short man's memory is. Soon after Russia moves against Israel, the Antichrist will walk purposefully into a political vacuum to become a worldwide dictator. Jerusalem will watch that man walk onto the stage of world history as a man of peace only to become Hitler incarnate.

Israel's False Messiah—the Antichrist

And in the latter time of their kingdom,
When the transgressors have reached their fullness,
A king shall arise,
Having fierce features,
Who understands sinister schemes (Dan. 8:23).

The Antichrist is a real, physical human being. Though some have hypothesized that the Antichrist, or Beast, will be a system or a computer, the Bible leaves us no doubt that he is a *person*.

In Matthew 24 Jesus said there would be many antichrists, or "false christs," who would come. But there is one unique, anointed of hell, brilliant, charismatic, articulate world leader who will arise at the dawn of the Tribulation and baptize the world in a river of blood. The Bible calls him the "son of perdition" (2 Thess. 2:3), which translates to "the chief son of Satan."

I believe that just as God waited for the fullness of time before He sent His Son to be born of a virgin, the people of the earth are awaiting the appearance of the Antichrist. Look around. Jesus had John the Baptist to shout, "Prepare the way of the LORD!" (Matt. 3:3) and we have many who are preparing the world for the advent of Antichrist.

Recently my daughter Christina, a junior at Oral Roberts University, burst into my bedroom and said, "Dad, you've got to see this." She flipped the TV channel to CNN's coverage of Marilyn Manson, a man who professes to be a high priest in the church of Satan. The lyrics of his songs encourage rape, incest, body mutilation, murder, and Satan worship. He hates capitalism and believes fascism is America's hope for the future.

Is he successful? Very. His recordings hit "triple platinum" status as soon as they are released (that's over three million copies sold), and thousands of American young people jam stadiums and arenas for his concerts. Manson and his deceived legions are begging for Satan's messiah to rule the world. They will get their wish.

The organized church in America has become anti-Christ, or "against Christ." Consider:

- The church that denies the Bible to be the inspired, inerrant Word of God is anti-Christ. Jesus said, "I am the way, the truth, and the life" (John 14:6). John's Gospel states "Your word is truth" (17:17) and "In the beginning was the Word, and the Word was with God, and the Word was God. . . . And the Word became flesh and dwelt among us, and we beheld His glory, the glory as of the only begotten of the Father, full of grace and truth" (1:1, 14). If Jesus is *truth*, and the Word is *truth*, to deny truth is indeed anti-Christ!

- The church that ordains homosexuals is anti-Christ. If you believe that God approves of homosexuality, reconsider His urban renewal program for Sodom and Gomorrah.
- The church that denies the virgin birth is anti-Christ.
- The church that has "a form of godliness but [denies] its power" (2 Tim. 3:5) is anti-Christ.
- The church that denies that Jesus Christ is Lord is anti-Christ!

Forty years ago most people laughed at the concept of a human Antichrist. They're no longer laughing. Thousands of high school and college students in America today proudly wear the number 666 on their clothes and schoolbooks and have it tattooed on their bodies.

The practice and study of satanism have exploded in America. Our youth are taking oaths of allegiance to Satan and his coming messiah, the Antichrist. Rock music groups have adopted his name, and their concerts resemble nothing so much as a demonic worship service.

Wake up, America! The songs we're singing, the books we're reading, the movies we're watching are glorifying the Prince of Darkness and his coming Antichrist.

The Time of His Appearing

After Russia and its Arab allies are defeated, the Antichrist, Satan's messiah, will step out onto the world stage. The earth is prepared for him, the time is nearly upon us. I believe he could be alive right now. And just as Jesus knew He was God's Son, sent into the world to redeem men, I believe the Antichrist knows he is Satan's emissary, sent into the world to destroy as many human lives as possible.

Jesus warned that the times of the Antichrist will be by far the worst the world has ever known. In His discourse to the disciples regarding "the tribulation of those days" as recorded in Matthew 24, Mark 13, Luke 21, and John 16, He foretold a period of false messiahs, wars, rumors of wars, sorrow, deception, iniquity, persecution, and worldwide catastrophe. The end times would be so terrible, Jesus said, that "unless those days were shortened, no flesh would be saved" (Matt. 24:22).

An Impostor of Peace

This false messiah will present himself to the world as a man of peace. Perhaps he will be a Nobel Peace Prize winner. At the beginning of his allotted time, he will defeat and merge three kingdoms, demonstrating his power to influence and lead men. Daniel 8:25 says that by cunning he "shall destroy many." To illustrate his diplomacy and desire for peace, he will make a seven-year treaty with Israel, but he will break this agreement after only three and one-half years.

The Antichrist will be a man with hypnotic charm and charisma. Interestingly enough, historians record that when Hitler was in power, men were afraid to look into his hypnotic eyes. The Antichrist will have awesome demonic power to control world leaders with his hypnotic gaze and the force of his personality.

The Antichrist will come from the federated states of Europe, the revived Roman Empire. In his rise to power, he will be the leader of one nation in the ten-kingdom federation, then he will conquer three of the ten nations and become the Beast of Revelation 13:1, "having seven heads and ten horns, and on his horns ten crowns, and on his heads a blasphemous name." He will instantly assume dictatorial authority over nations, turning his ravenous gaze toward the apple of God's eye—Israel.

The Antichrist will use military force to gain and maintain world supremacy. Daniel wrote, "But in their place he shall honor a god of fortresses" (Dan. 11:38). Though he comes as a man of peace, he will bathe the world in blood before he gets to Armageddon where blood will flow to the depth of a horse's bridle for a distance of 200 miles (Rev. 14:20).

Initially, the Antichrist will bring world prosperity. The prophet wrote, "Through his cunning / He shall cause deceit to prosper under his rule" (Dan. 8:25). This suggests that there might be a worldwide economic collapse, and the man of sin, the Son of Perdition, the Chief Son of Satan, will seduce the world with the promise of prosperity.

One Money, One Religion, One Ruler

The Antichrist's three-point plan for world domination consists of a one-world currency, a one-world religion, and a one-world government now being called the New World Order.

His economy will be a cashless society in which every financial transaction can be electronically monitored. No one will be able to buy or sell without a mark sanctioned by the Antichrist's administration. Therefore, the Antichrist will force every person on earth to receive a mark in the right hand or the forehead. Without this mark, you will not be able to legally buy groceries or hold a job. Revelation 13:16–17 tells us, "He causes all, both small and great, rich and poor, free and slave, to receive a mark on their right hand or on their foreheads, and that no one may buy or sell except one who has the mark or the name of the beast, or the number of his name."

Technology has made it possible for every person on earth today to be electronically monitored. With the implantation of a small computer chip, painlessly installed and virtually invisible to the naked eye, where you go and what you buy can be monitored by the Global Positioning System. The GPS involves a small, handheld device that bounces a signal to a satellite and back to indicate a monitored individual's exact position. It is accurate to within ten feet and is presently used in jet aircraft, naval vessels, and criminal monitors.

We're already scanning our pets. Responsible dog and cat owners are urged to microchip their animals. One tiny computer chip, no bigger than a grain of rice, is injected between the animal's shoulder blades. It's invisible and virtually undetectable, until someone swipes a scanner over the spot where the chip lies. Suddenly the animal's identification number comes up on the scanner, and from that number whoever needs information has access to the pet owner's address, phone number, veterinarian, and any other pertinent information. It's amazing, but it's nothing compared to the program the Antichrist will implement.

Satan has been scheming to institute a new world order since Nimrod proposed to build a mighty tower on the plains of Shinar—the Tower of Babel. During Christ's temptation, Satan offered Jesus a new world order if He would bow down and worship him. After World War I, the "war to end all wars," President Woodrow Wilson helped found the League of Nations to uphold peace through a one-world government. Adolf Hitler told the German people he would bring a "new order" to Europe.

Sound familiar? The Antichrist will institute a one-world government far more successful than any that have gone before him. There will be no national borders in his world; the nations will be ruled by international law imposed upon them by international leaders. Communication? Easy on the World Wide Web. Authority? Supported by an international peacekeeping force, instituted by a world court. The elements are already in place; the world looks only for a leader, a new Caesar.

Idolatry in Jerusalem

The Antichrist will have an evil counterpart, the False Prophet. Together they will perform miracles, and the world will marvel. The world looks for miracles today in the same way some of the scribes and Pharisees of Jesus' day asked that He give them a sign to prove His divinity.

Miracles are not a sign of God's approval. But men are easily deceived, and they will see the signs and wonders performed by the False Prophet, and they will believe that the Antichrist is divine.

In an attempt to stop Jesus Christ, the rightful Heir, from reclaiming His throne in Jerusalem, the Antichrist will establish his capitol, his home, and his headquarters in God's Holy City. There he will set himself up as God, commanding the world to worship him. Those who do not worship him will be executed. Some theologians believe he will be homosexual, for Daniel 11:37 tells us, "He shall regard neither the God of his fathers *nor the desire of women,* nor regard any god; for he shall exalt himself above them all" (italics mine).

Jesus told His disciples that the Antichrist would demand worldwide worship. Matthew 24:15–16 records His warning: "'Therefore when you see the "abomination of desolation," spoken of by Daniel the prophet, standing in the holy place' (whoever reads, let him understand), 'then let those who are in Judea flee to the mountains.'"

The prophet Daniel wrote, "Then the king [Antichrist] shall do according to his own will: he shall exalt and magnify himself above every god, shall speak blasphemies against the God of gods, and shall prosper till the wrath has been accomplished; for what has been determined shall be done" (11:36).

John the Revelator explained it further: "Here is wisdom. Let him who has understanding calculate the number of the beast, for it is the number of a man: His number is 666" (Rev. 13:18). In the Bible, 6 is the number of sin. The number of the Antichrist is 666, meaning he is part of a threefold demonic trinity consisting of Satan, the Antichrist, and the False Prophet, who will work signs and wonders in the Antichrist's name to deceive the nations of the world. Many of them will believe that the Antichrist is God.

Why does the Antichrist demand to be worshiped? From the beginning, before Genesis 1:1, Satan has had a compulsion to be worshiped. Isaiah exposes Satan's sinister motives, saying:

> How you are fallen from heaven,
> O Lucifer, son of the morning!
> How you are cut down to the ground,
> You who weakened the nations!
> For you have said in your heart:
> "I will ascend into heaven,
> I will exalt my throne above the stars of God;
> I will also sit on the mount of the congregation

On the farthest sides of the north;
I will ascend above the heights of the clouds,
I will be like the Most High" (14:12–14).

Lucifer lusted for worship before the gates of Eden were open. This demonic compulsion drove Satan to tempt Jesus in the wilderness, saying, "All these things [the kingdoms of the world] I will give You if You will fall down and worship me" (Matt. 4:9). Satan's messengers now invite the world to worship the Prince of Darkness via music and moral rebellion against God.

During his reign on earth, the Antichrist will be the object of an assassination attempt. John says, "I saw one of his heads as if it had been mortally wounded, and his deadly wound was healed. And all the world marveled and followed the beast (Rev. 13:3). The Antichrist will be shot in the head and will miraculously recover, emulating the death and resurrection of Jesus Christ.

John records the prophecy of what will happen next: "And he [the False Prophet] deceives those who dwell on the earth by those signs which he was granted to do in the sight of the beast [the Antichrist], telling those who dwell on the earth to make an image to the beast who was wounded by the sword and lived. He was granted power to give breath to the image of the beast, that the image of the beast should both speak and cause as many as would not worship the image of the beast to be killed" (Rev. 13:14–15).

But the Antichrist will go too far. Revelation 13:6 tells us, "He opened his mouth in blasphemy against God, to blaspheme His name, His tabernacle, and those who dwell in heaven." As the Antichrist, Satan's messiah, stands on the plains of Megiddo, marshaling his massive army for the Battle of Armageddon, he will look into heaven at the angels who had the opportunity to follow him in his first rebellion against God. He will look at Christ, to whom Satan offered the kingdoms of the world. He will look up at the raptured believers who stand with their Lord, and he will say, "Look, all of you. Look where you would be if you had followed me. You would be rulers of the earth. I *forbid* God to send His Son to earth to reign. I am God here. I rule and reign in this city. Jerusalem is MINE!"

The Antichrist's End

Unlike Jesus Christ, whose throne will know no end, the Antichrist's days will be numbered. While God readies the armies of heaven, the nations of earth will rise against the Antichrist:

> At the time of the end the king of the South shall attack him; and the king of the North shall come against him like a whirlwind, with chariots, horsemen, and with many ships; and he [Antichrist] shall enter the countries, overwhelm them, and pass through. He shall also enter the Glorious Land, and many countries shall be overthrown. . . . But news from the east and the north shall trouble him; therefore he shall go out with great fury to destroy and annihilate many. And he shall plant the tents of his palace between the seas and the glorious holy mountain [Jerusalem]; yet he shall come to his end, and no one will help him (Dan. 11:40–41, 44–45).

We have met these kings of the North and South before. This time, as before, they represent a renewed Russian Empire conspiring with a pan-Islamic confederation to cleanse Jerusalem and seize control of the Middle East oil fields. The Antichrist has defeated these kings before, and he subdues them again. He is probably not too worried about their threat until he learns of the 200-million-warrior army (Rev. 9:16) advancing toward him from the east.

After hearing about the advancing eastern army, the Antichrist will advance from the territory of the twice-defeated king of the South to Armageddon, a natural battlefield, to face the armies from the North and the East.

And God, who has borne all the blasphemies He can bear, will say, "Son, take the armies of heaven—the angels, the Old Testament saints, the church—and return to earth as the King of kings and Lord of lords. Go and make Your enemies Your footstool. Go and rule the earth with a rod of iron. Go and sit upon the throne of Your father, King David."

Then will come the final invasion, not from the north, south, east, or west, but from heaven. It is the invasion described in Revelation 19, the attack led by Jesus Christ, the Lamb of God, the Lion of Judah, and the Lord of Glory!

Mounted upon a white horse, the King of kings will descend onto the battlefield at Armageddon. As He comes, His eyes are like blazing fire, and the armies of heaven follow Him on white horses. Out of the Messiah's mouth comes a sharp two-edged sword, the Word of God with which He created the world out of chaos, raised Lazarus from the dead, and rebuked the unruly wind and waves on the Sea of Galilee. His spoken word will crush His enemies in milliseconds.

Then shall the armies of the Antichrist and the kings of the earth gather to wage war against the Lion of Judah, who is mounted on His milk-white stallion and followed by His army wearing crowns and dazzling robes of white. I will be in that army, for it is composed of those who were raptured with the church and the loyal angels of God!

In Revelation 19:12, John wrote that Jesus had a name "written that no one knew except Himself." As a Jew, John knew that God appeared to Abraham, Isaac, and Jacob by the name of God Almighty, *El Shaddai*. But God did not reveal Himself to them by the name of Jehovah (*Yahweh*). The patriarchs knew God as the Almighty One, but they had no concept of Him as an intimate friend and Master, the One who delights to walk with His children "in the cool of the day" (Gen. 3:8) as God walked with Adam in the Garden of Eden.

Christ's robe, dipped in His innocent blood that was shed on the cross, is His prayer shawl. The tsitsit of His shawl in Hebrew spells "Jehovah God Is One," meaning He is the King of kings and Lord of lords.

"Then the beast [Antichrist] was captured, and with him the false prophet who worked signs in his presence, . . . These two were cast alive into the lake of fire burning with brimstone" (Rev. 19:20). The Antichrist who invaded Jerusalem, who murdered and killed righteous Jews who would not worship him, is cast alive and forever into the lake of fire. Hallelujah to the Holy One of Israel who shall rule and reign forever from Jerusalem. Of His kingdom there shall be no end.

CHAPTER 9

GLIMPSES OF THE FUTURE

The future is in the past.

Why is it so important for America to lock arms with the nation of Israel? The reasons are revealed in the biblical history of the Jewish people. America's fate depends upon our treatment of the nation of Israel. Look at the boneyard of human history. Examine the testimony of nations that had the opportunity to bless Israel but chose to curse Israel instead. Without exception, they experienced the judgment of God, sank into oblivion, and became historical footnotes in the annals of time. Their prosperity became poverty, their power replaced by international pity.

What About Tomorrow?

If you're concerned about prophecy for the future, the following pages will contain the most important clues you will find anywhere in the world. You could spend a lifetime researching libraries that will yield nothing more profitable than understanding the biblical basis of prophecy.

To know the future, you must master what the Bible tells you about the past. Everything God will do, He has done before.

In the movie *Back to the Future,* Marty McFly's DeLorean time machine fascinated millions of viewers. We applauded as Marty shot back through time in a matter of seconds. While some of us are intrigued to revisit our childhoods or investigate our ancestors, nothing the human imagination can conjure is equal to what God has already prepared to equip His people to read the future. Bible prophecy lifts the veil off tomorrow and shines the spotlight on what is to come.

Jesus and Joseph

If we study Joseph, the Old Testament champion who saved his father, his brothers, and his people from starvation, we can discover the hidden story of the Messiah. Theology calls this the principle of types and shadows. By studying one situation, life, or prophecy, we can glean truths and more deeply understand another situation.

Joseph enacted the future of Jesus Christ nearly 2,000 years before Jesus was born! Consider the startling similarities between the Hebrew ruler of Egypt and the Jewish Messiah.

- The names *Jesus* and *Joseph* come from the Hebrew root word for *salvation,* and each man was the means of saving grace to his people. God sent Joseph from his father's house to a strange land in order for his family to be fed in a time of drought and thirst, providing bread for the very brothers who betrayed him. God dispatched Jesus from the right hand of the Father to the earth as the "bread of life" (John 6:48) and "living water" (John 4:10).

- Joseph's brothers rejected and betrayed him. His siblings sold him into the hands of his enemies, and Jacob's favorite son became a slave. Jesus was betrayed by Judas, by Peter, by Thomas. The Bible tells us, "He came to His own, and His own did not receive Him" (John 1:11).

- Joseph's brothers sold him for twenty shekels of silver (Gen. 37:28), the common price of a slave. Judas sold Christ to the Pharisees for thirty pieces of silver (Matt. 26:15), the usual price of a slave.

- Joseph was falsely accused of rape by Potiphar's wife. Her lies sent him to prison (Gen. 39:19–20). Similarly, the Pharisees lied about Jesus' teaching, condemning Him to death. Because of false accusations, Jesus descended to the ultimate pit . . . death.

But there's more! Through an act of God, Joseph was released from prison and promoted to the palace where he sat at Pharaoh's right hand. Free of death's ultimate confinement and bondage, Jesus arose and ascended to the right hand of God the Father. At every point, Joseph walked the exact path Jesus trod generations later.

Read the Exodus story carefully and you'll discover that Joseph's brothers traveled to Egypt *three times* before the man who had worn the coat of many colors dropped his disguise. When Pharaoh's vizier dropped the masquerade and revealed himself, he said, "I am Joseph, your brother." His brothers wept openly and bitterly.

How does that aspect of Joseph's life translate to Jesus? The connection has to do with the land of Israel.

The first time the Jews entered the land under Joshua's leadership. After the Exile, the Hebrews entered the land a second time with Nehemiah in order to rebuild the walls of Jerusalem and reestablish the nation.

In 1948 the Jews entered Israel for the third time when the United Nations recognized their statehood. As foreseen by the prophet Isaiah, a nation was born in a day (66:8).

Just as Joseph revealed his identity to his brothers on their third visit, the last return of Israel in 1948 prepared the way for the revelation of the Messiah. As we examine the past, we know that immediately before us lies the moment when the people of Israel will discover the identity of Messiah. On the third visit, He will reveal Himself.

And, like Joseph's brothers, the children of Israel will weep openly and with bitter tears. Zechariah said, "They will look on Me [Jesus] whom they pierced. Yes, they will mourn for Him as one mourns for his only son, and grieve for Him as one grieves for a firstborn" (12:10).

When you understand Bible prophecy, you have the capacity to accurately anticipate the future. Biblical stories are a theology of hidden eschatology. Yesterday is a dramatic foreshadowing of the essence of tomorrow. Everything God will do, He has already done.

Joseph was a type, or foreshadow, of the Messiah. His shadow fell across the approaching centuries, leaving significant basic clues so others would recognize the Messiah when He came.

Seven Billboards Advertising Tomorrow

The prophetic principles of types and shadows are dramatically demonstrated in the seven great feasts of Israel. These annual events reveal a secret treasure of special insights to guide your decisions today.

The contemporary clues we need to understand the future are interwoven through the Leviticus 23. The chapter begins with this directive to Moses: "Speak to the children of Israel, and say to them: 'The feasts of the LORD, which you shall proclaim to be holy convocations, these are My feasts" (v. 2).

The Lord Himself established seven occasions of worship to guide Israel through the centuries until the Messiah comes. Christians often falsely assume these feasts are exclusively Jewish occasions. But the Bible makes it clear these days belong *to the Lord*. These feasts of the Lord are established for divine purposes, and everyone has a right to draw near.

Just as seven days finish a weekly cycle, seven festival occasions complete the work of God on earth. Each holiday was and is a trail marker pointing to the future. The seven feasts are:

1. The Feast of Passover
2. The Feast of Unleavened Bread
3. The Feast of Firstfruits
4. The Feast of Pentecost
5. The Feast of Trumpets (Rosh Hashanah)
6. The Feast of Atonement (Yom Kippur)
7. The Feast of Tabernacles (Sukkot)

Every year, observant Jews fulfill the cycle of remembrances and find renewed peace of mind. Once we've completed the same spiritual journey, we can understand why God rested after the sixth day of creation. God was not tired; He rested to teach us a divine principle. After the sixth day He rested, and, after the sixth feast the world will enter into 1,000 years of perfect peace and rest called the Millennium.

Each of the feasts of Israel points to and describes what lies ahead.

Stepping Stones to Splendor

Through His festivals, God gave us a dress rehearsal of what is ahead. The Hebrew word for feast, *mo'ed,* means "a set or appointed time." Of very similar meaning is *mikrah,* indicating "a rehearsal or recital." Each feast, like a dress rehearsal, offers a significant picture of the future. The combined seven feasts are a divine blueprint of what lies ahead for Jerusalem, Israel, and the rest of the world.

As we follow each holiday through the year, we are walking on God's pathway from here to eternity. While we cannot know "the day or the hour" of Jesus Christ's return to earth, we can reflect on the possible month for both the Rapture and the Second Coming. The date lies in the accumulative meaning of the seven feasts.

Remember the basic principle: Everything God will do, He has already done.

Through these seven events, God revealed His 7,000-year plan for humanity. The Bible says, "But, beloved, do not forget this one thing, that with the Lord one day is as a thousand years, and a thousand years as one day" (2 Peter 3:8). Every festival day represents one of God's millennial moments, and each feast is an indicator of a segment of heaven's special way to measure time.

When 6,000 years pass and the Sukkot moment has come, Jesus' 1,000-year reign will begin. We can forget the frustration we experienced every time we turned on the television and watched the evening news. We'll trade in the condom culture and politically correct madhouse for paradise. This AIDS-infected, abortion-loving, pornography-addicted, secular-humanist sewer will disappear as Jesus Christ redeems the entire creation.

The Two Appearances

How do we start calculating time on God's stopwatch? Israel's feasts occur during two different seasons, reflecting the two different appearances of Jesus Christ on the earth.

The first time He came as a suffering Savior. In the coming age, He will return as King of kings and Lord of lords.

The first time He came, He was dragged before Herod and Pilate. The next time He comes, Herod and Pilate will bow before Him, for "at the name of Jesus every knee should bow, of those in heaven, and of those on earth, and of those under the earth, and that every tongue should confess that Jesus Christ is Lord, to the glory of God the Father" (Phil. 2:10–11).

The first time He came, He was considered an insurrectionist too dangerous to live, and so He was crucified on a Roman cross. The next time He comes, He will sit on the throne of His father, King David (Luke 1:32), and of His kingdom there shall be no end.

The spring season has seen the suffering Savior. The fall season awaits the coming of the King of glory who will rule the earth with "a rod of iron."

The first four festivals take us from the beginning of spring to the gathering of the barley harvest. Passover, Unleavened Bread, Firstfruits, and Pentecost mark the passing of winter and the coming of summer.

The first of three fall festivals begins at the end of the wheat harvest. The Feasts of Trumpets, Atonement, and Tabernacles remind the Jews that winter is ahead.

The two sets of holidays also coincide with the two annual seasons of rain. Spring brings the former rain; the latter rain comes in the fall. The prophet Hosea knew the seasons and rain cycles were "insider information" pertaining to what lay ahead. He wrote, "He will come to us like the rain, / Like the latter and former rain to the earth" (6:3).

These holidays predict Jesus' coming by foreshadowing a chain of events leading up to His return!

Let's start with the feasts that occur in the season of the former rain and see what we can discover.

The First Festival:
The Feast of Passover

On the tenth day of A'bib (March or April on the English calendar), preparation for the annual Passover observance begins. The Lord demanded, "This month shall be your beginning of months; it shall be the first month of the year to you. Speak to all the congregation of Israel, saying: 'On the tenth of this month every man shall take for himself a lamb, according to the house of his father, a lamb for a household'" (Ex. 12:2–3).

For four days a one-year-old male lamb without blemish was tied close to the house so the family would know and remember the lamb like a beloved pet. At 3:00 in the afternoon, the father of the house laid his hand upon the head of the lamb and cut its throat. Then he applied the blood of innocence to the sides of the door and smeared it on the doorposts. The house was literally sealed with blood.

The family not only remembered but reenacted the death angel's fearsome journey through Egypt. The firstborn sons of the Egyptians died, but the houses of Israel were spared. Where there was lamb's blood, the angel passed over. If the door was not sealed with the animal's blood, the firstborn child would die that night.

On this extraordinary evening, Israel learned the meaning of redemption by blood. As is true today, the father was the spiritual leader of the house. If the father failed in his spiritual duty, death came to his children. When the faith of contemporary fathers falters, children still die spiritually, and often physically.

How did Passover signal the shape of the future? Jesus fulfilled the meaning of the Passover ritual. The moment John the Baptist saw Jesus, he exclaimed, "Behold! The Lamb of God who takes away the sin of the world!" (John 1:29). Jesus was God's male lamb, without spot or blemish.

Even Pilate cried out, "I find no fault in Him" (John 19:6). And just as the Passover lamb was put on public display, Jesus stood before Israel in the temple and was examined by the Pharisees. He was God's final offering to end the reign of sin and death over humanity.

Death Dies

On the fourteenth day of A'bib, A.D. 33, at the third hour (9:00 A.M.), Israel's high priest tied the lamb to the altar for sacrifice. At that exact moment outside the city walls of Jerusalem, Jesus, the Lamb of God, was nailed to the cross. For six hours both the lamb and Jesus awaited death. Finally, at the ninth hour (3:00 P.M.), the high priest ascended the altar in the temple and sacrificed the lamb. His words thundered out over the city of Jerusalem, "It is finished!"

On Calvary's stark mountain, God the Father, the final High Priest of all creation, placed His holy hand on the head of His only begotten Son, allowing the total sin of the world to descend upon Jesus. Barely able to lift His blood-spattered face toward heaven, Jesus shouted in triumph, "It is finished!" (John 19:30).

The past was the guide to the future. The Passover forever declared that God saves His people through the shedding of blood.

My friend, we, too, are redeemed by blood, but not by the blood of goats and bullocks. We are saved by the precious blood that flows from Immanuel's veins. Not the blood that streamed from the altar when Solomon slaughtered 22,000 animals while dedicating the temple. We are cleansed from all sin by the blood Christ offered once and for all on the cross. We are not saved by the blood of infants slain by Herod to prevent the coming of Christ, but through the blood that makes every demon in hell tremble with fear.

Passover is Israel's great celebration of freedom. It is a matter of historical fact that the Hebrews were owned by Pharaoh, not by Egypt. The unyielding tyrant cared nothing for God or man. His foolish arrogance hung around his neck like a millstone, finally sending him to his death in the depths of the Red Sea. When Pharaoh drowned, his death canceled his control over the slaves. His ownership of the Jews ended instantly and permanently.

Every year when Passover comes, God reminds His people that He is the only one who can set them free. You and I were slaves to sin and Satan. We lived in chains and in bondage to fear. When Jesus Christ became our Passover Lamb, He ended the reign of death in our lives. The Lamb of God shouted from the cross, "It is finished!" At that moment, we were liberated from death, hell, and the grave; we were liberated from the guilt of the past and the fear of tomorrow. Satan is forever a defeated foe. "Therefore if the Son makes you free, you shall be free indeed" (John 8:36).

God's prophetic stopwatch started running on the night of Passover, A.D. 33. As the hands sweep past the numbers of each hour of the day, His people know they can look to the future without fear or apprehension. We have assurance of what cannot yet be measured.

You can no longer be defeated by yesterday. There is no need for you to be afraid of tomorrow. God does not say, "I am the great I WAS." Nor does He say, "I am the great I WILL BE." You can live in joy and victory *today* for God declares, "I AM the great I AM" (see Ex. 3:14). He's the God of the present.

Passover was the first prophetic sign of what was to come. Its meaning was fulfilled at Calvary. One epoch lies behind us, but six yet remain.

The Second Festival: The Feast of Unleavened Bread

On the fifteenth day of A'bib, the night after the week-long Passover festival begins, the Feast of Unleavened Bread is observed. Jews eat roasted lamb, bitter herbs, and unleavened bread. In Jesus' day, the people ate the sacrificial lamb that had been killed the day before.

This Passover meal, called the seder, is itself a picture of the death and resurrection of Christ. In the middle of the ritual, a piece of matzo (unleavened bread that is striped and pierced in the baking process) is broken into three pieces. The second piece, the *Afikomen,* is wrapped in white linen and hidden away for a little while, then found amid great rejoicing.

What an incredible picture and prediction of how Jesus Christ, the Bread of Life, would be wounded with the stripes of a whip, pierced with a sword, wrapped in linen, and hidden away in a borrowed tomb. On the night Jesus was betrayed, He ate the Last Supper (so called because it was the last meal in which leavened bread could be eaten before the festival) with His disciples and told them that the bread was His body that was to be broken for them.

Just as the matzo at the Feast of Unleavened Bread is without leaven, Jesus was without sin. His body was hidden away for three days, but then He rose and reappeared on the earth amid great rejoicing.

Before the feast can begin, the house must be cleansed of all leaven. Leaven, or yeast, makes the bread rise, and a practicing Jewish family will literally sweep the house clean to make certain there is no leaven on the premises. (Israel's kosher army will actually "sell" all of its warehouses, granaries, government food supplies, military cooking and eating equipment to a non-Jewish employee until after Passover.[1])

The heavenly Father decreed that any Jew eating leavened bread during this period should be cut off from the people (Ex. 12:15). Why was His judgment so strong? Because in the Bible, leaven is the type, or metaphor, for sin. Leaven represents the pride and arrogance that lead men to feel they have no need of God. Jesus said, "Take heed and beware of the leaven of the Pharisees and the Sadducees" (Matt. 16:6), and Paul added, "Your glorying is not good. Do you not know that a little leaven leavens the whole lump?" (1 Cor. 5:6).

The message of this feast? God has zero tolerance for sin.

Just like yeast, sin puffs us up. The Bible warns that our sins will always find us out, and the wages of sin is death. The Scriptures speak plainly about sin, for we are not only held responsible for our sinful acts, but we will be held accountable for the good deeds we neglected to do. "Therefore,"

James wrote, "to him who knows to do good and does not do it, to him it is sin" (4:17).

America, wake up. The Feast of Unleavened Bread warns us of an important eternal fact—no one can escape God's measuring stick. Nonobservant Jews were "cut off," or killed, for disobedience. We are no different. Tragically, too many Americans have forgotten that God hasn't changed His mind about the seriousness of sin.

During the past forty years secular humanism has stripped any sense of absolute right and wrong from American minds. Our children now live by "lifeboat" ethics. With the Ten Commandments exiled from our classrooms by the Supreme Court, and the ACLU seeking freedom *from* religion, our students no longer believe in sin. Liars are excused as being "extroverted" or "imaginative." Adultery is now "free love." Through the National Endowment for the Arts, our government feels free to use our tax money to pay artists to depict Jesus on a cross in a glass of urine. Why not? Nothing is sacred anymore in America.

Four thousand babies are murdered every day in America's abortion mills. Partial-birth abortion, a thoroughly repugnant practice, is more common than the experts would have you believe. The spreading culture of death spews blood and gore into our living rooms as week after week television offers an unending buffet of murder and mayhem.

To make matters worse, our political leaders are marching at the front of the parade leading to the moral abyss. The Clinton administration sells a night in the Lincoln bedroom to the highest bidder while China puts on a full-court press to subvert America's democratic process. In the halls of Congress, legislators peddle influence like souvenirs. Shame has no meaning!

How can a politician have sky-high approval ratings while swimming in one major scandal after another? He can't, unless there is no standard of righteousness, no concept of sin, no notion of honor, no understanding of integrity. Without these things, the country quickly sinks into the darkness of moral blindness. No one is listening to the Bible's warning that "righteousness exalts a nation, / But sin is a reproach to any people" (Prov. 14:34).

What's gone wrong in America? The church is certainly part of the problem. We're the embarrassment. The "greasy grace" preached from pulpits across this land set the stage for our brain-dead morality. People wink at sin and transgress with smiles on their faces. The self-satisfied settle back and smugly salve their consciences with a quick quip: "I'm covered by grace."

Let me tell you something, dear friend—greasy grace only forgives the sin. God's grace forgives the *sinner*. If you want to be truly forgiven and a new creation, go to God, not to those who will tell you that "slipping up" is only natural and to be expected. Quit trying to analyze your sin and just confess it.

Let me remind you of the eternal facts: Grace was never intended to be a license to sin. Extending forgiveness to anyone without demanding change in their conduct makes the grace of God an accomplice to evil. To the woman caught in adultery, Jesus said, "Go and sin no more." He expected her to change. He still expects transformation. Friends, pay attention to the Feast of Unleavened Bread. God has zero tolerance for sin.

God would have spared Sodom and Gomorrah if He could have found just ten righteous people within those walls. But because of the total moral collapse, He annihilated the entire society. Do you think God is going to make an exception for America? The eyes of God are studying our society this very moment. If the day comes when He can't find enough people to retard the moral and spiritual rot, God will crush this nation as well.

America's best national defense policy does not lie in producing more stealth bombers, manufacturing more condoms, propounding more sex education, or providing more clean needles for drug addicts. Our only hope lies in a revival of the righteousness of God to sweep this nation. America will either have a revival of righteousness or rebellion in the streets.

The Third Festival: The Feast of Firstfruits

On the sixteenth day of A'bib, immediately after the Feast of Unleavened Bread, the Feast of Firstfruits commemorates the day Israel went down into the depths of the Red Sea and came out the other side alive. The children of Israel marched into a watery grave and God raised them on the other bank a nation of free people. Little did they know they were also demonstrating how God would bring salvation to the entire world!

The Feast of Firstfruits is a foreshadowing of the work of both Good Friday and Easter, a type of the death and resurrection of Jesus Christ. Paul wrote, "But now Christ is risen from the dead, and has become the firstfruits of those who have fallen asleep [the dead]" (1 Cor. 15:20).

Jesus explored the chambers of death. He arose on the third day and announced, "I am the resurrection and the life. He who believes in Me, though he may die, he shall live. And whoever lives and believes in Me shall never die" (John 11:25–26). There is no spiritual death for the believer. Though his body may die, his spirit lives on with Christ.

Just as Israel marched out of the jaws of death (the Red Sea) to stand on solid ground, Jesus Christ arose the victor over death, hell, and the grave. Just as Jesus predicted, He arose the mighty conqueror over powers and principalities. Rome could not convict Him, the Cross could not conquer Him, and the grave could not contain Him. He is alive this very moment at the right hand of God, awaiting the hour of His second coming when kings, queens, presidents, and prime ministers shall bow at His feet and confess that He is Lord, to the glory of God the Father.

The Fourth Festival: The Feast of Pentecost

On the second day of Si'van (May or June on the English calendar), exactly fifty days after the Feast of Firstfruits, the commemoration of the giving of the Law begins. Following the Exodus and the Hebrews' miraculous escape from the Red Sea where Israel traveled until they reached the foothills of Mount Sinai, God instructed Moses to have the people purify themselves. At the end of their forty-seven-day journey, they purified themselves for three days, resulting in a total of fifty days, hence the word *pentecost*. Fearfully and faithfully they approached Mount Sinai, the great mountain of God, to receive the Ten Commandments.

As Moses went up to speak with God, the ground shook and a mighty rushing wind roared over the desert plain. Fire glowed on the mountaintop. According to Jewish tradition, when God spoke to Moses, He not only spoke in Hebrew, but in every known tongue on earth. But something more happened in this story.

The stage was set for the future and God's mission to reach the entire Gentile world. Prophecy was written into the plot. God was doing exactly what He was going to do fifty days after the resurrection of Jesus Christ!

Keeping the story of the Hebrews at Sinai in mind, let's look at the story of Pentecost found in the book of Acts. Every aspect of that first Pentecost was duplicated as 120 faithful followers of Jesus gathered in the Upper Room, the site of Jesus' last supper. Ten people, a minyan, was the number required by Jewish law to have a kosher prayer meeting. Ten representatives for the twelve tribes of Israel (totaling 120) huddled together, trying to understand why Jesus had commanded them to "tarry in the city of Jerusalem until you are endued with power from on high" (Luke 24:49). As they prayed together, they joined together in one mind, one heart, and one spirit. Suddenly Moses' experience on Mount Sinai was duplicated again.

A rushing mighty wind filled the Upper Room. Tongues of fire rested on their heads just as fire rested on the crest of Mount Sinai. Days earlier Jesus had promised His followers, "But you shall receive power when the Holy Spirit has come upon you" (Acts 1:8).

Empowerment came in awesome ways. Just as God spoke on Mount Sinai in every known language, even so the disciples spoke in every known language in the Upper Room. The fire about Mount Sinai foreshadowed the coming power of Pentecost.

Paul proclaimed, "For the kingdom of God is not in word but in power" (1 Cor. 4:20). The gospel of the empty tomb is a story of power. Let no one mistake the message. There is power in His name, power in His gospel, power in His blood, and power in His church. If the apostles wanted to sing a contemporary hymn in the Upper Room, they couldn't have chosen a better one than "All hail the power of Jesus' name! Let angels prostrate fall; bring forth the royal diadem, and crown Him Lord of all!"

The purpose of Pentecostal power is evangelism. "But you shall receive power when the Holy Spirit has come upon you; and you shall be witnesses to Me" (Acts 1:8). The top priority of every Christian is to be a soul winner, and Solomon assured us that "he who wins souls is wise" (Prov. 11:30). The first evidence of supernatural power is soul winning. Without that, Christians are trees without fruit, wells without water, and clouds without rain.

Don't Miss the Dress Rehearsal

The feasts of the "former rain," consisting of Passover, Unleavened Bread, Firstfruits, and Pentecost, are acts one, two, three, and four in God's last-minute preparations for the divine drama of the Second Coming. The prophetic counterparts to these feasts are behind us, their roles fulfilled.

The hands on God's clock are swiftly moving. As the first four feasts predicted what is now past, so the next festivals help us calculate what lies ahead.

The Fifth Festival:
The Feast of Trumpets (Rosh Hashanah)

Rosh Hashanah, the first day of the Jewish civil year, begins on the first of the seventh month, Tis'ri—September or October on the English calendar. According to Jewish custom, this is the date on which God created Adam, the first man. This is also called the Day of Judgment, when God sits on His throne and determines the destiny of each individual in the year ahead. In order to show trust in God's compassion, Jews dress in their best for this festival, usually in white, to signify purity, and celebrate the day with joy.[2]

Rosh Hashanah, the Feast of Trumpets, fulfills the Lord's command to Moses: "Speak to the children of Israel, saying: 'In the seventh month, on the first day of the month, you shall have a sabbath-rest, a memorial of blowing of trumpets, a holy convocation" (Lev. 23:24).

The "blowing of trumpets" refers to the shofar, the ram's horn that is blown exactly 100 times during the Rosh Hashanah service. Moses Maimonides, a Jewish scholar, explains the rationale behind the trumpet blowing:

> Although the sounding of the shofar on Rosh Hashanah is [observed because it is] a decree of the Torah, still it has a deep meaning, as if saying: "Wake up from your deep sleep, you who are fast asleep . . . search your deeds and repent; remember your Creator."[3]

While the first four festivals occur in close proximity, an entire season passes before the fall commemoration of trumpets begins. (See page 181—"The Jewish Calendar.")

This long period represents the dispensation of grace we now live in. Of all the feasts, this is the only time span in prophecy that cannot be exactly determined. The incalculable period is the one we're living in, the period of time where we wait for the angels to blow God's great trumpet that will call the Bride of Christ to her mansions on high.

The trumpets of God are the most important signal the world can possibly receive. Rosh Hashanah is a type of the Rapture of the church, a time that is drawing very near.

What is the Rapture? In 1 Corinthians 15:51–52, Paul wrote, "Behold, I tell you a mystery: We shall not all sleep, but we shall all be changed—in a moment, in the twinkling of an eye, at the last trumpet. For the trumpet will sound, and the dead will be raised incorruptible, and we shall be changed."

The Jewish Calendar

Month	Day	Festivals	Meaning of Word	English Months
1. A'bib	10th	Selection of Passover Lamb	Green Ears	March/ April
	14th	Passover		
	15th-21st	Unleavened Bread		
	16th	Firstfruits		
2, I'Jar			Brightness	April/ May
3. Si'van	6th	Pentecost		May/ June
4. Tam'muz				June/ July
5. Ab			Fruitful	July/ August
6. E'lul			Good for Nothing	August/ September
7. Tis'ri	1st	Trumpets	Flowing Rivers	September/ October
	10th	Day of Atonement (Yom Kippur)		
	15th-21st	Feast of Tabernacles (Sukkot)		
8. Mar-chesh'van			Rain	October/ November
9. Chis'leu				November/ December
10. Te'beth				December/ January
11. She'bat				January/ February
12. A'dar			Fire	February/ March

Paul explained the mystery of the Rapture, the next event on God's prophetic calendar. At the sound of God's trumpet, believers who have died will come out of the grave to be raised incorruptible, with new, supernatural, immortal bodies. Those who have not yet died a physical death will be caught up in the clouds to meet Jesus Christ. This mass ingathering of believers, the Bride of Christ, is commonly called the Rapture.

In explaining His return, Jesus left us with a paradox. On one hand, He said, "But of that day and hour no one knows, not even the angels of heaven, but My Father only" (Matt. 24:36). On the other hand, we *can* know that He "is near—at the doors!" (Matt. 24:33).

How can we know that He is near? A clue is found in Matthew 24:38–39: "For as in the days before the flood, they were eating and drinking, marrying and giving in marriage, until the day that Noah entered the ark, and did not know until the flood came and took them all away, so also will the coming of the Son of Man be."

Noah lived in a situation very similar to ours. God had issued a warning, a call to repentance, and He had told Noah to prepare and be ready. Noah obeyed. Even though he didn't know the exact time the Flood would come, He knew it was near, even at the door, because God put him, his family, and the animals on the boat and personally closed the door. Noah didn't know the exact moment the rains would fall and the fountains of the deep would be opened, but he knew without any doubt that the time was near.

We know, from signs of Bible prophecy such as those detailed in my book *Beginning of the End,* that the end is near. Without a doubt, we are the terminal generation.

When will the Rapture of the church take place? I believe it may happen at the Feast of Trumpets.

The Mystery of the Last Trumpet

Great confusion exists in Christian circles over the meaning of the Feast of Trumpets. Sincere people have missed the real meaning of Paul's instruction about the Rapture when he wrote, "We shall all be changed—in a moment, in the twinkling of an eye, at the last trumpet" (1 Cor. 15:51–52).

Some theologians reason that if there is a "last trump" there has to be a series of trumpets. The only series of trumpets mentioned in the New Testament is described in Revelation 8—9, so these theologians surmise that the church will go through the Great Tribulation. (Note: I have put together a series of studies featured in the *John Hagee Prophecy Bible* that explain in great detail why Christians will not go through any part of the Tribulation.)

If Gentile theologians are to get on track, they must understand the Jewish roots of our faith. The answer lies in what happened in the ancient Jewish wedding ceremony. Follow closely the nuptial chain of events:

In a traditional ancient ceremony, the hopeful bridegroom went to the home of his potential bride carrying three things: his best financial offering, a betrothal contract, and a skin of wine. If the father was impressed and accepted the bridegroom's offering, he called the daughter for her response. If things were acceptable to her, the bride-to-be drank the wine, and immediately a trumpet sounded to announce their betrothal.

During the following year of betrothal, the couple could not see each other alone, and a chaperone always accompanied them wherever they went. During this year, the bridegroom went to his father's house to prepare a place, a *chupah,* or honeymoon bed.

No engraved invitations were sent out for the wedding. If people preparing the calendar wanted to reserve a day for the celebration, they had a problem. When the young bridegroom was asked for the date of his wedding, he could only reply, "No man knows except my father." Why? Because he could not go get his bride until the father approved of his son's preparation.

The bride, therefore, had to be in a state of constant readiness lest the bridegroom's arrival catch her by surprise. Often she kept a light burning in the window and an extra jar of oil on hand, lest the bridegroom come in the night and find her unprepared.

When the groom's father decided everything was in place and released his son to go fetch his bride, a second trumpet was blown. This trumpet, to announce the groom's coming, was called the "last trump." Thus announced, the bridegroom took the marriage contract to present to the father of his intended bride. He claimed her as his bride and took her from her father's house to his father's house. His father would be waiting to receive the couple, and then the groom's father would take the hand of the bride and place it in the hand of his son. At that moment, she became his wife. That act was called the *presentation*.

After the presentation, the bridegroom would bring his bride to the place he had gone to prepare. There he would introduce her to all the society of his friends who had heard the trumpet and come to celebrate the marriage at the marriage feast. In 2 Corinthians 11:2, Paul wrote to the church, "For I am jealous for you with godly jealousy. For I have betrothed you to one husband, that I may present you as a chaste virgin to Christ."

What a powerful picture of what God has prepared for us. We are the betrothed bride of Christ, purchased at Calvary with His precious blood. Paul said, "For you were bought at a price" (1 Cor. 6:20). The Almighty Father looked down from heaven and accepted the price of our redemption. We, the bride, accepted the Groom and the evidence of His love for us.

In this interim, as we wait between Pentecost and Trumpets, Jesus Christ, our Bridegroom, returned to His Father's house to prepare everything for our arrival. Before He departed this earth, Jesus said, "In My Father's house are many mansions; if it were not so, I would have told you. I go to prepare a place for you. And if I go and prepare a place for you, I will come again and receive you to Myself; that where I am, there you may be also" (John 14:2–3).

How do we accept the proposal of Christ? Just like the bride, each time we take the Communion cup and drink the wine, we proclaim our wedding vows to our beloved Lord. We demonstrate that we love only Him, that we are loyal to Him, and that we are waiting for Him. Like the eager bride, we keep our lamps burning and strive to be ready, for we don't know when He might come.

Our Bridegroom *will* soon come for us. Make no mistake, we must wait with our ears attuned to hear the last trumpet sound.

We're not going into or through the Tribulation. We're going home, to the city where there will be no death, no parting, no sorrow, no sickness. We're going to the city where the Lamb is the Light, to the city where roses never fade, to the city inhabited by Abraham, Isaac, Jacob, and King Jesus.

The primary function of the Feast of Trumpets is to ask us one question: Are we prepared for the summons that will come when the world least expects it? Just as the blast of the shofar awakens the Jews and urges them to search their deeds and remember their Creator, the blast of the Lord's trumpet will awaken us to the realization that the Bridegroom has come.

Are you ready?

The Judgment Seat of Christ and the Bridegroom's Wedding Reception

What happens after the bridegroom takes his bride home? She must stand before him and await his appraisal. If she is wise, she has prepared a trunk with her wedding clothes, and she will adorn herself in beautiful garments that she has prepared because of her love for her bridegroom.

In biblical times the marriage feast was a celebration to honor not the bride, as is our custom, but the bridegroom. All the guests who assembled at the marriage banquet were expected to compose poems and sing songs to honor him as they appreciated the beauty and grace of his bride.

The Blessed Bridegroom has been presented with a bride, and now He is coming to display the bride to all His friends, not that they might honor the bride, but that they might honor the Bridegroom because of the bride's beauty. Jesus will be honored, not because of what we are, but because of what He has made us. Writing in Ephesians, Paul refers to this analogy when he wrote that Christ gave Himself for the church so that "He might present her to Himself a glorious church, not having spot or wrinkle or any such thing, but that she should be holy and without blemish" (5:27).

We're not holy by nature. We're not holy by practice. But the bride is the Father's love gift to the Son to honor the Son for His obedience to the Father's will. When Jesus, the Bridegroom, is presented with His bride, He will say, "She is beautiful, without spot or wrinkle." He will rejoice to lead her to the marriage banquet.

Imagine this, if you will: The bridegroom takes the bride into his chamber, looks her in the eye, and says, "Now I will take you in to meet all my friends. They will want to praise you, to exclaim over your beauty. So look into your hope chest and pull out those garments you have prepared for our marriage feast." What would you do if you looked into your hope chest and found nothing? Or perhaps you found only slipshod, poorly prepared garments? You would be embarrassed before your loving bridegroom, his father, and the assembled witnesses.

Soon after the Rapture, we Christians will stand before the Judgment Seat (sometimes called the "Bema Seat") of Christ. While Jesus took the full weight of God's judgment of sin for us, we must still stand before God for a final review of our faithfulness. As the nations of the world rise and fall because of their morality, our personal decisions and actions are creating evidence for the coming judgment on us. We will either receive crowns and commendation or reproof and reprimand. Our garments will either be designed to glorify our Bridegroom, or they will appear as filthy rags. The issue won't be salvation, because this judgment takes place in heaven with the redeemed. The qualities under examination will be our character and faithfulness.

In 1 Corinthians 3:11–15, Paul wrote:

> For no other foundation can anyone lay than that which is laid, which is Jesus Christ. Now if anyone builds on this foundation with gold, silver, precious stones, wood, hay, straw, each one's work will become clear; for the Day will declare it, because it will be revealed by fire; and the fire will test each one's work, of what sort it is. If anyone's work which he has built on it endures, he will receive a reward. If anyone's work is burned, he will suffer loss; but he himself will be saved, yet so as through fire.

On display at the Bema Seat will be five great crowns for the loyal and trustworthy servants of Christ who were faithful until death. To steadfast believers tested by prison and persecution even to the point of death, God will give a Crown of Life (Rev. 2:10). A never-fading, never-tarnishing diadem awaits the self-sacrificing pastor-shepherds of the flock (1 Peter 5:2–4). Everyone who ran life's race with patient endurance and perseverance will receive a Crown of Righteousness (2 Tim. 4:8). Evangelists and soul winners can eagerly anticipate receiving the Crown of Rejoicing (1 Thess. 2:19–20). Finally, all who overcome will be handed a wonderful Victor's Crown (1 Cor. 9:25).

Which crown will you wear?

Will you take your Bridegroom's arm with the scent of smoke upon you? Or will you join Him, dressed in white, with a glowing crown upon your head? John warns all believers, "Hold fast what you have, that no one may take your crown" (Rev. 3:11). Run the race to win!

The Sixth Festival:
The Feast of Atonement (Yom Kippur)

On the tenth day of Tis'ri (September or October), the day of Yom Kippur, Israel comes together in worship, self-examination, reflection, and repentance. This is the most sacred day of the Jewish year. In ancient times it was the only occasion when the high priest entered the Holy of Holies, and a scapegoat bearing the sins of Israel was sent off to Azazel in the wilderness (Lev. 16:10).[4] On this day, righteous Jews must come to grips with their lives.

Daniel knew how extremely significant this feast would be in God's plan for the future. In Daniel 9:24, the prophet recorded the significance of the sixth feast:

Seventy weeks are determined
For your people and for your holy city [Jerusalem],
To finish the transgression,
To make an end of sins,
To make reconciliation for iniquity [Yom Kippur],
To bring in everlasting righteousness,
To seal up vision and prophecy,
And to anoint the Most Holy [Jesus Christ].

Just as the Crucifixion corresponded to the fulfillment of Passover down to the last detail, the Scripture points to the incredible promise of what will happen on this day, the Second Coming of Jesus Christ. Which Yom Kippur? No one knows "the day or the hour," but we know His coming is near, even at the door.

The second coming of Jesus Christ—and I'm not talking about the Rapture, where Jesus appears in the clouds without touching the earth—should occur 2,520 days, or seven prophetic years of 360 days, after the day Israel signs a seven-year peace accord with the Antichrist. The treaty signing will come after this extraordinary man emerges as the predominant leader of the European Union or a country or confederation that was once part of the Roman Empire. He will be the Beast described in Revelation 13:1, the creature who rises from the sea with "seven heads and ten horns, and on his horns ten crowns, and on his heads a blasphemous name." Ten crowns with seven heads of state indicate that three nations of his confederation have fallen under his control.

Although Israel will consider this thoroughly evil man to be the messiah, he will be Hitler reborn. His reign of evil influence will end, however, when Jesus Christ, Messiah, comes to destroy him. He will fulfill the intent of Yom Kippur, the day of reconciliation between people and God and His chosen people.

Yom Kippur's Meaning for the Church

The true bride of Christ will be gone by the time the Antichrist appears, but Yom Kippur reminds us that the church should be preaching repentance just before the Rapture. The last word Jesus Christ gave to the church was not the Great Commission. His last word to the church was *repent.*

In the first chapters of Revelation, Christ gave John the Revelator a message for seven churches of Asia. Five out of those seven churches were told to repent. I believe every detail in Scripture has a divine purpose. If five out of seven churches in Asia needed to repent, I believe five out of seven churches and five out of seven believers in America need to repent.

Repentance is the key to revival in America. We will either have national repentance and revival or revolution in the streets.

The Seventh Festival:
The Feast of Tabernacles (Sukkot)

The Feast of Tabernacles, or Sukkot, is held by divine decree (Lev. 23:39) on the fifteenth through twenty-first days of Tis'ri, which falls in September or October. Sukkot begins after the ingathering of the harvest, and is the happiest of the biblical festivals. It celebrates God's bounty in nature and God's protection, symbolized by the fragile booths in which the Israelites dwelled in the wilderness. According to Jewish tradition, Sukkot is also a festival involving Gentiles, and seventy bullocks were offered up in the temple for the seventy nations of the world (all they knew existed in that time). In the messianic age, the Jews believe, all nations will come up to Jerusalem to celebrate Sukkot as an affirmation of faith in God's guidance of the world.[5]

As seven is the number of fulfillment and completion, this festival ushers in God's rest and points to the 1,000-year Millennium, the reign of Christ.

The Feast of Tabernacles is also called the Feast of Lights. The ancient custom in Israel during the festival was to place four great candelabra in the midst of the temple. Their large bowls were full of oil, and their wicks were made of holy garments the priests had worn during the preceding year. Everyone in Jerusalem could see the light.[6] How fitting that Jesus stood in the midst of the people and proclaimed, "I am the light of the world" (John 9:5).

We find our identity in Jesus Christ. He demonstrated who we are and what we are to be doing. The Bible urges us, "Let your light so shine before men, that they may see your good works and glorify your Father in heaven" (Matt. 5:16). Light reveals, exposes, and finally conquers darkness. We are to be the light in a dark world, just as Christ was.

Hear this! There can be no peaceful coexistence between light and darkness. "What communion has light with darkness?" asks the apostle Paul (2 Cor. 6:14). The time has come for the church of Jesus Christ to stop complaining about the darkness and turn on its light!

Don't whine. *Shine!*

Victory doesn't come without a fight. There is no sunrise without a night. There is no purchase without a cost. There is no crown without a cross. Don't curse the darkness, turn on the light.

Joy Unspeakable

The Feast of Tabernacles is also called "the season of our joy." I believe Jesus was born during the time of Sukkot. He was not born in December, for Luke 2:8 records that at the time of Jesus' birth there were "shepherds living out in the fields, keeping watch over their flock by night." From biblical times to the present, shepherds in Israel leave the cold of the open fields and pen their sheep up at night beginning in the month of October. Due to the nighttime cold, there were no shepherds in any fields in December. It was customary, however, to send flocks out after Passover, and they would remain in the fields until the first rain or frost in October. Jesus' birth, then, had to occur sometime between Passover and early October. I believe He was born during the season of Sukkot, the season of joy!

The angels gathered on the first Christmas morning and announced, "Do not be afraid, for behold, I bring you good tidings of great joy which will be to all people" (Luke 2:10). They knew the King of kings had come into the world. In the same way, the Feast of Sukkot celebrates the coming time when Jesus Christ will rule over the entire earth.

Zechariah prophesied that the Messiah would be God's greatest gift to the earth. "And the LORD shall be King over all the earth," he wrote, "In that day it shall be— / 'The LORD is one,' / And His name one" (14:9). The Messiah's coming will bring joy to the nations.

Jesus Christ is our joy. As we await His second coming when He will rule over the entire world, we rejoice in the power of the name that is above every name. One of the given names of Jesus, *Immanuel,* means "God with us." He is the wonderful Counselor, the mighty God, the everlasting Father, and Prince of Peace. Our Savior and Deliverer is also our Friend and Comforter. He gives us joy today that the world will know tomorrow. In His presence is the fullness of joy.

CHAPTER 10

THE FINAL DAWN OVER JERUSALEM

Nearly 250 years ago, the English writer Isaac Watts wrote a hymn based upon Psalm 98. Although we traditionally sing his song at Christmas, the lyrics are really about the Millennial reign of Christ:

> Joy to the world! The Lord is come;
> Let earth receive her king;
> Let every heart prepare Him room,
> And heaven and nature sing.

> Joy to the earth! The Savior reigns;
> Let men their songs employ;
> While fields and floods, rocks, hills and plains,
> Repeat the sounding joy.

> No more let sins and sorrows grow,
> Nor thorns infest the ground;
> He comes to make His blessings flow
> Far as the curse is found.

> He rules the world with truth and grace,
> And makes the nations prove

The glories of His righteousness,
And wonders of His love.[1]

Jerusalem, that blessed city, will be the capitol of Jesus Christ when He rules in the Millennium, the 1,000-year reign of God upon the earth. For the first time in centuries, Jerusalem will rest securely, not fearing its enemies.

What Is the Millennial Kingdom?

Scripture has much to say about the Millennium. It is known in Scripture as "the world to come" (Heb. 2:5), "the kingdom of heaven" (Matt. 5:10), "the kingdom of God" (Mark 1:14), "the last day" (John 6:40), and "the regeneration" (Matt. 19:28). Jesus told His disciples, "Assuredly I say to you, that in the regeneration, when the Son of Man sits on the throne of His glory, you who have followed Me will also sit on twelve thrones, judging the twelve tribes of Israel" (Matt. 19:28).

The Millennium was foreshadowed in the Old Testament by the Sabbath, a time of rest. A rest was to be observed after six workdays, six workweeks, six work months, and six work years. In God's eternal plan, the earth will rest after 6,000 years as well, as He ushers in the Millennial Kingdom of the Messiah.

During the Millennium, the geography of Israel will be changed. Israel will be greatly enlarged and the desert will become a fertile plain. For the first time Israel will possess all the land promised to Abraham in Genesis 15:18–21. A miraculous river will flow east to west from the Mount of Olives into both the Mediterranean and the Dead Sea. But it will be "dead" no longer!

Listen to how Zechariah described it:

And in that day His feet will stand on the Mount of Olives,
Which faces Jerusalem on the east.
And the Mount of Olives shall be split in two,
From east to west,
Making a very large valley;
Half of the mountain shall move toward the north
And half of it toward the south.
Then you shall flee through My mountain valley. . . .
And in that day it shall be
That living waters shall flow from Jerusalem,
Half of them toward the eastern sea
And half of them toward the western sea;
In both summer and winter it shall occur. . . .

All the land shall be turned into a plain from Geba to Rimmon south of Jerusalem. Jerusalem shall be raised up and inhabited in her place from Benjamin's Gate to the place of the First Gate and the Corner Gate, and from the Tower of Hananel to the king's winepresses.

The people shall dwell in it;
And no longer shall there be utter destruction,
But Jerusalem shall be safely inhabited. . . .

And it shall come to pass that everyone who is left of all the nations which came against Jerusalem shall go up from year to year to worship the King, the LORD of hosts, and to keep the Feast of Tabernacles (14:4–5, 8, 10–11, 16).

Jerusalem, the apple of God's eye, will become the joy of the world. The city will become the international worship center, and people from all over the world will make pilgrimages to worship in the holy temple. Kings, queens, princes, and presidents shall come to the Holy City so "that at the name of Jesus every knee should bow, of those in heaven . . . and that every tongue should confess that Jesus Christ is Lord, to the glory of God the Father" (Phil. 2:10–11).

The prophet Micah wrote of the Millennial Kingdom, and the poetry of his verse has inspired many a public building (including the United Nations Building) to be inscribed with a portion of his words. But Micah wasn't writing about the United Nations, he was writing about God's Millennial capitol, Jerusalem:

> Now it shall come to pass in the latter days
> That the mountain of the LORD's house
> Shall be established on the top of the mountains,
> And shall be exalted above the hills;
> And peoples shall flow to it.
> Many nations shall come and say,
> "Come, and let us go up to the mountain of the LORD,
> To the house of the God of Jacob;
> He will teach us His ways,
> And we shall walk in His paths."
> For out of Zion the law shall go forth,
> And the word of the LORD from Jerusalem.
> He shall judge between many peoples,
> And rebuke strong nations afar off;
> They shall beat their swords into plowshares,
> And their spears into pruning hooks;
> Nation shall not lift up sword against nation,
> Neither shall they learn war anymore (4:1–3).

The Holy City, now six miles in circumference, will occupy an elevated site and will be named *Jehovah-Shammah,* meaning "the Lord is there" (Ezek. 48:35) and *Jehovah Tsidkenu,* meaning "the Lord our righteousness":

> In those days Judah will be saved,
> And Jerusalem will dwell safely.
> And this is the name by which she will be called:
> THE LORD OUR RIGHTEOUSNESS (Jer. 33:16).

Millennial Judgment

After the Tribulation, the first thing God will do in the Millennial Kingdom is gather the nations of the earth and judge them for the manner in which they treated the nation of Israel. With the sound of the archangel and the blast of the trumpet, Jesus Christ is going to descend again to the Mount of Olives. The sides of the mountain will split in half, Jesus will walk across the Kidron Valley to enter the temple mount through the golden gate. At that moment, the Lion of Judah will assemble the divine tribunal and begin calling the nations to the bar of justice to answer for their abuse or blessing of the Jewish people and the State of Israel.

The arrogant and mighty men of war will grovel in the dust. The proud will beg for pity. Tyrants who showed Israel no mercy will plead for compassion. Generals and field marshals will attempt to hide behind lame excuses. The world will watch as God humbles and humiliates emperors, kings, and kingdoms. This is the judgment of nations.

Haman and his seven sons will march before the Lamb's bench for justice. During the days of the Babylonian exile, this treacherous demagogue sought to annihilate the Jewish people. Only the skillful intervention of Esther saved them. Even though the plot backfired and Haman was hanged, his trial will not be finished until God exposes him before the assembly of nations and angels escort him into the lake of fire.

Waiting in the wings will be Adolf Hitler, Heinrich Himmler, and every gestapo officer who worked in a Nazi death camp. Joseph Stalin and Nikita Khrushchev will stand behind them. When the holy gavel pounds on the Carpenter's bench, Hitler will bow in the presence of the Rabbi from Nazareth and plead for his very existence.

Nazi soldiers will have to explain how they could weep before statues of the Virgin Mary, who was Jewish, on Sunday and throw her descendants into gas chambers on Monday.

The Vichy government of France that cooperated with the monstrous Nazi death machine will cry out in sorrow because they betrayed the Jewish people. Lenin will rush forward, and Joseph Stalin will answer for decades of Russian anti-Semitism.

God does not forget. He will remember the six million Jews slaughtered in the Holocaust, one by one, to the Polish creators of the Auschwitz ovens. Stripe for stripe, wound for wound, a complete accounting will continue until God has rectified every crime committed against His people. In a single stroke, He will mete out mercy and judgment.

The British Empire will be called to the judgment bar for their White Paper Policies during World War II and before. As Hitler was killing 25,000 people a day, multitudes of Jews tried to escape. Yet the British White Paper Policy allowed only 5,000 Jews a year to immigrate to Israel. Israel, under control of the British, returned helpless Jews to Hitler's death camps. The British captured Jews sneaking into Israel in leaky ships. The British closed the gates of mercy on Jews trying to escape. Almighty God will remember their actions on this judgment day.

The Great White Throne Judgment

But individuals will be judged as well as nations. The Great White Throne Judgment, where sinners stand in the presence of a holy God, is one of the most awesome revelations given to man in the Word of God. In Revelation 20:11, John wrote, "Then I saw a great white throne and

Him who sat on it, from whose face the earth and the heaven fled away. And there was found no place for them."

The judgment at the Great White Throne takes place after the Millennial reign is completed. It is held in an intermediate place, somewhere between heaven and earth. It could not take place on the earth, for the earth will be under renovation. It could not occur in heaven because sinners would never be permitted in the presence of a holy God.

There are two resurrections—the resurrection of the just, and the resurrection of the unjust. The resurrection of the just takes place in three phases. The first phase was at Calvary when men came out of their graves and were seen in the city of Jerusalem. The second phase will be at the Rapture of the church. The third phase will be in the middle of the Tribulation, where martyred saints are taken into heaven.

All men, both righteous and unrighteous, will experience a resurrection day. In John 5:27–29, Jesus says that the Father "has given Him authority to execute judgment also, because He is the Son of Man. Do not marvel at this; for the hour is coming in which all who are in the graves will hear His voice and come forth—those who have done good, to the resurrection of life, and those who have done evil, to the resurrection of condemnation."

In Revelation 20:12, John continues to describe the Great White Throne Judgment, saying, "And I saw the dead, small and great, standing before God, and books were opened. And another book was opened, which is the Book of Life. And the dead were judged according to their works, by the things which were written in the books."

Notice that God has two sets of books. The first book, the Book of Life, contains the name of every person who accepted Jesus Christ while they were on the earth. When the wicked dead approach the Great White Throne, God will first look for their names in the Book of Life. Obviously, they will not be there.

Then He will open the books that are His written records of every word, thought, and deed of the wicked dead. The result? "And anyone not found written in the Book of Life was cast into the lake of fire" (Rev. 20:15).

In which judgment will you appear? Will you stand before the Judgment Seat of Christ where the works of believers are tried by fire, or the Great White Throne Judgment for those who have rejected Jesus Christ? The choice is yours.

The New Jerusalem: God's Golden, Glorious City

After the Millennium, when Satan and his followers have been eternally banished to the lake of fire, God will renovate this present world. He will then present us with a new heaven and a new earth, to which a *New Jerusalem* will descend from heaven. The apostle John described it in the closing chapters of the Revelation:

> Now I saw a new heaven and a new earth, for the first heaven and the first earth had passed away. Also there was no more sea. Then I, John, saw the holy city, New Jerusalem, coming down out of heaven from God, prepared as a bride adorned for her husband. And I heard a loud voice from heaven saying, "Behold, the tabernacle of God is with men, and He will dwell with them, and they shall be His people. God Himself will be with them and be their God.

"And God will wipe away every tear from their eyes; there shall be no more death, nor sorrow, nor crying. There shall be no more pain, for the former things have passed away." . . .

Then one of the seven angels who had the seven bowls filled with the seven last plagues came to me and talked with me, saying, "Come, I will show you the bride, the Lamb's wife." And he carried me away in the Spirit to a great and high mountain, and showed me the great city, the holy Jerusalem, descending out of heaven from God, having the glory of God. Her light was like a most precious stone, like a jasper stone, clear as crystal. Also she had a great and high wall with twelve gates, and twelve angels at the gates, and names written on them, which are the names of the twelve tribes of the children of Israel: three gates on the east, three gates on the north, three gates on the south, and three gates on the west. Now the wall of the city had twelve foundations, and on them were the names of the twelve apostles of the Lamb. And he who talked with me had a gold reed to measure the city, its gates, and its wall. The city is laid out as a square; its length is as great as its breadth. And he measured the city with the reed: twelve thousand furlongs [about 1,400 miles]. Its length, breadth, and height are equal. Then he measured its wall: one hundred and forty-four cubits [about 200 feet], according to the measure of a man, that is, of an angel. The construction of its wall was of jasper; and the city was pure gold, like clear glass. The foundations of the wall of the city were adorned with all kinds of precious stones: the first foundation was jasper, the second sapphire, the third chalcedony, the fourth emerald, the fifth sardonyx, the sixth sardius, the seventh chrysolite, the eighth beryl, the ninth topaz, the tenth chrysoprase, the eleventh jacinth, and the twelfth amethyst. The twelve gates were twelve pearls: each individual gate was of one pearl. And the street of the city was pure gold, like transparent glass.

But I saw no temple in it, for the Lord God Almighty and the Lamb are its temple. The city had no need of the sun or of the moon to shine in it, for the glory of God illuminated it. The Lamb is its light. And the nations of those who are saved shall walk in its light, and the kings of the earth bring their glory and honor into it. Its gates shall not be shut at all by day (there shall be no night there). And they shall bring the glory and the honor of the nations into it. But there shall by no means enter it anything that defiles, or causes an abomination or a lie, but only those who are written in the Lamb's Book of Life.

And he showed me a pure river of water of life, clear as crystal, proceeding from the throne of God and of the Lamb. In the middle of its street, and on either side of the river, was the tree of life, which bore twelve fruits, each tree yielding its fruit every month. The leaves of the tree were for the healing of the nations. And there shall be no more curse, but the throne of God and of the Lamb shall be in it, and His servants shall serve Him. They shall see His face, and His name shall be on their foreheads. There shall be no night there: They need no lamp nor light of the sun, for the Lord God gives them light. And they shall reign forever and ever (21:1–4, 9–27; 22:1–5).

Who will live in this Holy City? The holy angels, Christians who have placed their faith and trust in Christ, and redeemed Israel. Although the New Jerusalem is a wedding present from the Bridegroom to His bride, Israel is invited to dwell within these beautiful walls.[2]

In Hebrews 11, the roll call of faith, the author testifies of Jewish saints who placed their faith in God and obeyed His commands. They are invited to dwell in His heavenly city: "But now they desire a better, that is, a heavenly country. Therefore God is not ashamed to be called their God, for He has prepared a city for them" (v. 16).

Perhaps the most crucial occupant of heaven and the Holy City is Jesus Christ. He is the source, the strength, and the center of heaven.[3] By what right does He rule and reign over this Holy City?

Let's look back to the Abrahamic covenant. God promised Abraham, "I will make you exceedingly fruitful; and I will make nations of you, and kings shall come from you" (Gen. 17:6). God revealed how He planned to eventually rule over all the earth—through a king of His own appointment.

In Genesis 49 Jacob the patriarch called his twelve sons around his bed to give them a final blessing and to speak a prophetic word over each of them. His word over Judah is especially interesting:

Judah, you are he whom your brothers shall praise;
Your hand shall be on the neck of your enemies;
Your father's children shall bow down before you. . . .
The scepter shall not depart from Judah,
Nor a lawgiver from between his feet,
Until Shiloh comes (vv. 8, 10).

The word *Shiloh* may be rendered "He whose right it is to rule." Jacob thus prophesied that a king would come out of Judah's lineage who had the right to expect to be king.

In 2 Samuel 7:16, God made another promise, this one to King David: "And your house and your kingdom shall be established forever before you. Your throne shall be established forever." There are three important words in this verse:

house, kingdom, and *throne.* "Your house" is the descendants of David who would sit on his throne. "Your kingdom" is the kingdom of Israel. "Your throne" is his royal authority, the right to rule as God's representative. Twice in this one verse God told David that his dynasty, kingdom, and throne would last forever.

The last time I visited Jerusalem, I stood at the Shrine of the Book and stared for a long moment at the Dead Sea Scrolls. An overpowering feeling descended upon me—*those scrolls may have been touched and read by our blessed Lord.* It is one thing to think of Christ as a historical figure, a remote Savior who died 2,000 years ago and now sits at the right hand of the Father. It is quite another thing to walk the streets where He walked, to see items and objects that He might have held in His hands.

He was a man, but more than that, He is the King who will reign over Jerusalem forever. The throne of Jerusalem is His birthright.

The Gospel of Matthew opens with God breaking a silence of more than 400 years. Matthew gave Israel the message of the coming King by opening with a genealogy of Jesus Christ, "the Son of David, the Son of Abraham." If Jesus Christ is the son of Abraham, He is the Promised One through which all families of the earth should be blessed (Gen. 12:3). If Jesus Christ is the Son of David, He is the One who has the right to rule. He is Shiloh!

The angel of the Lord appeared to the Virgin Mary and said, "Do not be afraid, Mary, for you have found favor with God. And behold, you will conceive in your womb and bring forth a Son, and shall call His name JESUS. He will be great, and will be called the Son of the Highest; and the Lord God will give Him the throne of His father David. And He will reign over the house of

Jacob forever, and of His kingdom there will be no end" (Luke 1:30–33).

Jesus Christ was born, lived as a Jewish rabbi, and was crucified on a Roman cross. When Jesus ascended into heaven, God the Father said to Him,

Sit at My right hand,
Till I make Your enemies Your footstool (Matt. 22:44).

God is now preparing the nations for the last days. Jerusalem, who has suffered so much, stands on the brink of the greatest darkness it has ever known, but it will break forth into glorious light.

The nations of the world will gather in the Valley of Jehoshaphat for the Battle of Armageddon, when the nations meet the Son of God coming in the clouds of glory followed by His angels and the church triumphant.

John describes the sight, saying, "Now I saw heaven opened, and behold, a white horse. . . . [Messiah's] eyes were like a flame of fire, and on His head were many crowns" (Rev. 19:11–12). Why many crowns? Because He is "KING OF KINGS AND LORD OF LORDS" (Rev. 19:16). He is Shiloh, whose right to rule is given and guaranteed by God Almighty. He is the Son of David, and of His kingdom there shall be no end.

The citizens of Jerusalem, that ancient city that has seen so much suffering, will surrender streets that have flowed with blood for streets of pure gold. The desert sun will yield to the light of the Lamb, and the hatred of warring nations to the peace of God. The protective walls of Jerusalem, which were built and rebuilt with much toil and struggle, will be replaced by walls designed solely for beauty and glory. The Tree of Life, not seen or enjoyed since Eden, will grow in the center of the city. Nations will no longer look upon Jerusalem with jealousy or resentment but will look to it for the light of God's glory.

O Jerusalem, city of God, whose very dust and stones are loved by the faithful! The winds of war are fast approaching and bringing deep darkness. But by divine decree, the darkness will surrender to a beautiful and eternal dawn over Jerusalem.

On that final dawn over Jerusalem, when the Lamb who is the Light shall take His throne, there will be no more tears, no more pain, no more darkness.

Hallelujah! Joy to the world!

Notes

FOREWORD
1. Benjamin Disraeli, *Tancred,* bk. 3, ch. 4, *The Columbia Dictionary of Quotations,* licensed from Columbia University Press. Copyright © 1993, 1995 by Columbia University Press.

CHAPTER ONE
1. Seymour M. Hersh, *The Samson Option* (New York: Random House, 1991), p. 8.
2. "Attack—and Fallout," *Time,* June 22, 1981.
3. "A Vote Against Israel," *Newsweek,* June 19, 1981.
4. *The Congressional Record,* October 14, 1968, p. 31636.

CHAPTER TWO
1. John Phillips, *Exploring the World of the Jew* (Chicago: Moody Press, 1988), p. 128.
2. David Allen Lewis, *Israel and the USA, Restoring the Lost Pages of American History: The Story of Haym Salomon, Forgotten Patriot* (Springfield, MO: Menorah Press, 1993), pp. 3–10.
3. David Allen Lewis, *op. cit.,* p. 10.
4. Vendyl Jones, *Will the Real Jesus Please Stand?* (Tyler, TX: Priority Publishing, Institute of Judaic-Christian Research, 1983), pp. 220–28).
5. John Adams quoted in Rabbi Joseph Telushkin's *Jewish Wisdom* (New York: William Morrow and Company, 1994), p. 498.
6. *The Columbia Dictionary of Quotations* is licensed from Columbia University Press. Copyright © 1993, 1995 by Columbia University Press. All rights reserved.
7. *The Concise Columbia Encyclopedia* is licensed from Columbia University Press. Copyright © 1995 by Columbia University Press. All rights reserved.
8. Dr. Yoav Tenembaum, "The Last Romantic Zionist Gentile," © January 1996, *Jewish Post of New York Online.*
9. Dr. Yoav Tenembaum, *op. cit.*
10. *The People's Chronology* is licensed from Henry Holt and Company, Inc. Copyright © 1995, 1996 by James Trager. All rights reserved.
11. Theodore Roosevelt quoted in Rabbi Joseph Telushkin's *Jewish Wisdom, op. cit.,* p. 499.
12. Albert Einstein quoted in *The New York Times,* February 16, 1930.
13. *The People's Chronology* is licensed from Henry Holt and Company, Inc. Copyright © 1995, 1996 by James Trager. All rights reserved.

14. Émile Zola, *L'Aurore,* February 22, 1898, quoted in Rabbi Joseph Telushkin's *Jewish Wisdom, op. cit.,* p. 496.
15. Rabbi Joseph Telushkin, *op. cit.,* p. 498.
16. David Aikman, "For the Love of Israel," © 1996, Strang Communications.
17. David Aikman, *op. cit.*
18. Pope John XXIII quoted in Rabbi Joseph Telushkin's *Jewish Wisdom, op. cit.,* p. 469.
19. John Phillips, *op. cit.,* p. 129.

CHAPTER THREE
1. John Phillips, *op. cit.,* p. 111.
2. Dagobert Runes, *The War Against the Jew* (New York: Philosophical Library, 1968), p. 114.
3. John Phillips, *op. cit.,* pp. 115–16.
4. Mark Twain, *Harper's* magazine, September 1898.
5. *The New York Times,* December 21, 1996, p. A5.

CHAPTER FOUR
1. David Lloyd George quoted in Rabbi Joseph Telushkin's *Jewish Wisdom, op. cit.,* pp. 499–500.
2. Dagobert Runes, *op. cit.,* p. 106.
3. Malcolm Hay, *The Roots of Christian Anti-Semitism* (USA: Anti-Defamation League of B'nai B'rith and Alice Ivy Hay, 1981), p. 20.
4. Story of Hadrian contained in Lamentations Rabbah 3:9, quoted in Rabbi Joseph Telushkin's *Jewish Wisdom, op. cit.,* p. 463.
5. Malcolm Hay, *op. cit.,* p. 24.
6. Malcolm Hay, *op. cit.,* p. 26.
7. Chrysostom, Homily 4:1.
8. Malcolm Hay, *op. cit.,* p. 42.
9. Chrysostom, Homily 6:5 and 1:6.
10. Chrysostom, Homily 6:4.
11. Chrysostom, Homily 6:2, 6:4, 1:7, and 6:6.
12. Malcolm Hay, *op. cit.,* pp. 36–37.
13. Malcolm Hay, *op. cit.,* p. 37.
14. Jonathan Riley-Smith, ed., *The Oxford Illustrated History of the Crusades* (New York: Oxford University Press, 1995), p. 81.
15. Jonathan Riley-Smith, *op. cit.,* p. 39.
16. Jonathan Riley-Smith, *op. cit.,* p. 34.
17. Malcolm Billings, *The Cross & the Crescent: A History of the Crusades* (New York: Sterling Publishing Co., Inc., 1990), p. 15.
18. Malcolm Billings, *op. cit.,* p. 15.

19. Malcolm Billings, *op. cit.*, p. 16.
20. Malcolm Billings, *op. cit.*, p. 17.
21. Dagobert Runes, *op. cit.*, p. 37.
22. Malcolm Hay, *op. cit.*, p. 37.
23. Malcolm Billings, *op.cit.*, p. 66.
24. Rabbi Joseph Telushkin, *Jewish Wisdom, op. cit.*, p. 467.
25. Dagobert Runes, *op. cit.*, p. 34.
26. *Encyclopedia Judaica* (Jerusalem: Keter Publishing House, 1978), vol. 10, p. 114, and vol. 4, p. 64.
27. Malcolm Hay, *op. cit.*, p.37ff.
28. John Phillips, *op. cit.*, p. 113.
29. Edward Burman, *The Inquisition, Hammer of Heresy* (New York: Dorset Press, 1984), p. 135.
30. Edward Burman, *op. cit.*, p. 138.
31. Dagobert Runes, *op. cit.*, p. 87.
32. Edward Burman, *op. cit.*, p. 148.
33. Malcolm Hay, *op. cit.*, p. 160.
34. John Phillips, *op. cit.*, p. 112.
35. Malcolm Hay, *op. cit.*, p. 167.
36. Malcolm Hay, *op. cit.*, p. 167.
37. *Encyclopaedia Judaica*, vol. 11 (Jerusalem: Keter Publishing House Jerusalem Ltd., 1971), pp. 584–85.
38. *Encyclopedia Judaica*, vol. 3, *op. cit.*, p. 103.
39. Malcolm Hay, *op. cit.*, p. 169.
40. Malcolm Hay, *op. cit.*, p. 8.
41. Dagobert Runes, *op. cit.*, p. 114.
42. Malcolm Hay, *op. cit.*, p. 11.
43. Malcolm Hay, *op. cit.*, p. 3.
44. John Toland, *Adolf Hitler* (New York: Doubleday & Company, 1978), p. 326.
45. John Toland, *op. cit.*, p. 803.
46. John Toland, *op. cit.*, p. 331.
47. John Toland, *op. cit.*, p. 331.
48. John Toland, *op. cit.*, p. 617.
49. John Toland, *op. cit.*, p. 687.
50. John Toland, *op. cit.*, p. 287.
51. Nuremberg War Trials Staff, *Trial of the Major War Criminals, Before the International Military Tribunal: Nuremberg 14 November 1945– 1 October 1946*, vol. I, (Buffalo, NY: William S. Hein & Co., 1996), p. 50.
52. Nuremberg War Trials Staff, *op. cit.*, p. 251.
53. Nuremberg War Trials Staff, *op. cit.*, p. 439.
54. Nuremberg War Trials Staff, *op. cit.*, pp. 318–19.

55. John Toland, *Hitler, the Pictorial Documentary of His Life* (New York: Doubleday & Company), p. 287.

56. *The People's Chronology* is licensed from Henry Holt and Company, Inc. Copyright © 1995, 1996 by James Trager. All rights reserved.

57. D. M. Panton, "The Jew God's Dial," *Dawn*, August 15, 1924, pp. 197–201.

58. Malcolm Hay, *op. cit.*, p. 9.

59. Hyam Maccoby quoted in Rabbi Joseph Telushkin's *Jewish Wisdom, op. cit.*, p. 468.

60. Nikolay Berdyaev quoted in Rabbi Joseph Telushkin's *Jewish Wisdom, op. cit.*, p. 469.

61. Malcolm Hay, *op. cit.*, p. 116.

62. Malcolm Hay, *op. cit.*, p. 120.

63. Malcolm Hay, *op. cit.*, p. 121.

64. Malcolm Hay, *op. cit.*, p. 117.

65. Geoffrey Chaucer, *The Works of Geoffrey Chaucer*, ed. by F. N. Robinson (Boston: Houghton Mifflin Company, 1957), pp. 162–64.

66. Tomáš Masaryk quoted in Rabbi Joseph Telushkin's *Jewish Wisdom, op. cit.*, p. 497.

67. Malcolm Hay, *op. cit.*, p. 138.

68. Jeff Stein, "Hate on the Net," *Charlotte Observer*, August 24, 1997, pp. C1, 4C.

69. Geoffrey Chaucer, *op. cit.*, p. 162 (spelling modernized).

70. Voltaire's quote from his *Dictionnaire Philosophique* quoted in Rabbi Joseph Teluskin's *Jewish Wisdom, op. cit.*, p. 471.

CHAPTER FIVE

1. Malcolm Hay, *op. cit.*, p. 11.

2. Malcolm Hay, *op. cit.*, p. 20.

3. Malcolm Hay, *op. cit.*, p. 20.

4. Chaim Potok, *Wanderings* (New York: Fawcett Crest, 1978), p. 263.

5. Chaim Potok, *op. cit.*, p. 265.

CHAPTER SIX

1. Lucy Dawidowicz, *The War Against the Jews* (New York: Bantam Books, 1975), p. 27.

2. Malcolm Hay, *op. cit.*, p. 24.

3. Earl Paulk, *To Whom Is God Betrothed?* (Atlanta, GA: K-Dimension Publishers, 1985), p. 40.

4. Walter C. Kaiser Jr., Peter H. Davids, F. F. Bruce, and Manfred T. Brauch, *Hard Sayings of the Bible* (Downers Grove, IL: InterVarsity Press, 1996), pp. 569–70.

5. Kaiser, Davids, Bruce, and Brauch, *op. cit.,* p. 570.

CHAPTER SEVEN

1. Elie Wiesel quoted in *Writers at Work,* 8th ser., ed. George Plimpton, 1988.

CHAPTER EIGHT

1. Moris Farhi, *The Last of Days,* (New York: Kensington Publishing Corporation, 1983), p. 201.

2. Ibrahim Sarbal, leader of the Islamic Jihad Movement in Palestine— al Aqsa Brigades. Quote is provided by the Anti-Defamation League of B'nai B'rith.

3. Quote provided by the Anti-Defamation League of B'nai B'rith.

4. Joan Peters, *From Time Immemorial* (New York: Harper and Row Publishers, 1984), pp. 391–412.

5. Mitchell G. Bard and Joel Himelfarh, *Near East Report Myths and Facts* (Washington, D.C.: 1992), p. 308.

CHAPTER NINE

1. David C. Gross, *How to Be Jewish* (New York: Hippocrene Books, 1991), p. 145.

2. Alan Unterman, *Dictionary of Jewish Lore and Legend* (London: Thames and Hudson, Ltd., 1991), p. 168.

3. Rabbi Joseph Telushkin, *Jewish Wisdom, op. cit.,* p. 387.

4. Alan Unterman, *op. cit.,* p. 208.

5. Alan Unterman, *op. cit.,* pp. 191–92.

6. Ralph Gower, *The New Manners and Customs of Bible Times* (Chicago: Moody Press, 1987), p. 358.

CHAPTER TEN

1. Isaac Watts, "Joy to the World," *The Broadman Hymnal* (Nashville: Broadman Press, 1940), p. 137.

2. H. L. Willmington, *The King Is Coming,* (Wheaton, IL: Tyndale House, 1988), p. 300.

3. Willmington, *op. cit.,* p. 301.